psychic
surgery

psychic surgery

TOM VALENTINE

HENRY REGNERY COMPANY—CHICAGO

Quotation on page 119 is from the book *Powers That Be* by
Alexander Cannon. Copyright, 1935, by E. P. Dutton & Co.,
Inc., publishers, and used with their permission.

Contents

Foreword
by Harold Sherman
author of
Wonder Healers of the Philippines

Tom Valentine takes up in his *Psychic Surgery* where my *Wonder Healers of the Philippines* leaves off. I, too, was a reporter, and my assignment, as was Tom's, was to describe as accurately and truthfully as possible what I had personally witnessed and experienced, as well as documented case histories of many who had undergone psychic surgery operations by one or more of the Filipino spiritist healers.

Tom and I both came across evidences of fraud, performed apparently when the mysterious power exercised by the healers was not functioning through them, for whatever reason. But as I stated in my book and as Tom reaffirms in his, a single undeniable case of bare-handed psychic surgery proves the existence of a "white crow." All crows, from that time on, cannot be black. It is regrettable, of course, that fraudulent practices occur, but there have been false practitioners and counterfeiters in practically every walk of life. This fact should not lead to blanket condemnation of all professional people or healers as phony operators.

In reading Tom's compellingly interesting account of his investigation of psychic surgery, I was caused to relive in memory my experiences on the two trips I made to the Philippines, in 1966 and 1967, to study the work of the highly controversial Tony Agpaoa and other healers. There was great similarity in our adventures because Tom found fundamentally the same conditions. The phenomenon is difficult to believe even when you see it. But when a certain percentage of people with all manner of afflictions show marked improvement, if not definite recovery, after submitting to bare-hand surgery, you have to be impressed.

In *Psychic Surgery* Tom tells of a dramatic incident that occurred during my second trip to the Philippines (see chapter in *Wonder Healers of the Philippines* entitled "Your Mysterious

Powers of ESP") when James Osberg, a Chicago newspaper-
man, tried to make peace with the Filipino police authorities
and the medical examiners so that psychic surgeons threatened
with arrest could be freed to operate on some 111 desperately
ill terminal cases who had been flown to the Philippines by
chartered plane from the Detroit area.

I was present at the meeting, at Cresta Ola Beach, on the
South China Sea, during which Osberg offered to submit his
body to be opened by a psychic surgeon as proof that such an
operation, declared a hoax, was genuine. All Osberg asked in
return was that the police and medical examiners would sign
immunity from arrest of all psychic surgeons if the authenticity
of this type of surgery was demonstrated.

The challenge was rejected because the medical board members declared that even if such an operation were performed
(which they did not concede was possible), they would still
have to arrest the operator since he would be "practicing medicine without a license."

In recounting this experience Tom Valentine names names,
as he does throughout his fearlessly and forthrightly written
book. He also reports an interview with an investigator for the
American Medical Association, who also contacted me, and
whose predetermined prejudice against the phenomenon of
psychic surgery kept him from going to the Philippines to see
for himself or involving any qualified medical team to conduct
a fair and unbiased examination.

What Tom and I deeply deplore and find difficult to understand is the tendency of many scientists, doctors, and surgeons
to condemn, without investigation, anything new or unorthodox
in the way of healings. They fear the discovery, as in the case of
acupuncture, scorned and ridiculed for years, that it may exist
and may have value.

I used to look, a bit enviously, upon all scientists as "men
with open minds." It was thrilling to contemplate their access,
on the frontiers of science, to new inventions, new techniques,
and new knowledge, which would be of increasing benefit to

mankind. How disillusioning it was for me to discover that the scientists are often the most close-minded people of all!

As a "sensitive" in the field of extrasensory perception, I have submitted, at one time or another, as have many psychically endowed people, to investigation under laboratory conditions imposed by scientists. When successful results have been obtained, some scientists have remained reluctant to accept them as evidence of genuine phenomena; they look for explanations such as conscious or unconscious trickery or just good "guesswork."

Thus far, psychic surgery has not been subjected to laboratory testing, although some of the healers have been willing to come to this country for demonstration purposes. They would do this, however, at the risk of being arrested, not necessarily for fakery but for practicing medicine without a license.

I have often stated, in my published works and public comments, that I cannot and will not recommend that anyone go to the Philippines for psychic surgery. Despite the fact that some people have been healed, there is no guarantee that the next person may be. Anyone who decides to try psychic surgery must do so on his own responsibility. I know that Tom Valentine joins me in this declaration.

I ask all skeptics and members of the medical profession who still maintain that psychic surgery is a gigantic hoax: conceding the existence of some fraudulent practices, *how do you explain the healings?*

Much exists in this universe which would be wholly impossible within the framework of your present philosophy. Fortunately, these things do not require your knowledge or belief in order to exist. If you will but listen, have patience, and maintain scientific openmindedness, you will profit immeasurably. All things will eventually yield to full understanding, but you must devote your life to that end.

Eklal Kueshana
The Ultimate Frontier

1 The Phenomenon

HIS HANDS broke right through my skin, as if it were no thicker than water, and he poked around inside me with his fingers. I didn't feel any pain. I was wide awake; I could raise my head up and look right at his hands squishing my blood around, but I didn't feel a thing. Then he pulled this big hunk of tissue out of me—right before my eyes. He grinned and showed it to me, then casually tossed it into a wastebasket."

This is a firsthand account, by Irene Przybycien, of "psychic surgery" performed by Antonio C. Agpaoa, more commonly known as Tony, who has gained international fame as the greatest of many Filipino spiritualist healers.

In the Philippine Islands today there are many healers who claim the phenomenal ability to perform psychic surgery. These practitioners and their followers claim that the human body is opened for surgery without the use of instruments; only the bare hands of the healer touch the patient. The psychic surgeon uses no anesthetic. The patient is fully conscious but feels no pain. No antiseptics or sanitary precautions are needed, though conditions in the primitive chapels in which this incredible profession is practiced are worse than unsanitary. No cases of infection incurred during psychic surgery have been reported. Furthermore, these healers are said to diagnose "psychically" with unfailing accuracy. Thousands of cures of supposedly incurable diseases have been claimed.

By all acceptable standards such claims are preposterous. Upon hearing of psychic surgery, most people are amazed more by the fact that such a thing is believed by anyone in modern times than by the claims themselves. Most Americans who have heard of the phenomenon consider it a form of quackery, as it has been described by the American Medical Association in various magazine articles.

But if it is true, there comes the invariable question: "If this sort of thing is true, why isn't it generally known and accepted?"

The question is valid. It would be nice at this point to make a firm statement concluding that psychic surgery is 100 percent true, and orthodox dogma is 100 percent wrong. But it's not like that; the solution is not black and white but a thousand shades of gray.

Many people visit the Filipino healers with baffling, often incurable ailments and return fully cured. Such people are testimony to the truth of this phenomenon. In the Chicago area alone there are nearly 200 home movies of psychic operations taken by friends and relatives of patients. Though they are amateurish, many of these films vividly show barehanded surgical opening and tissue removal. Movies are not proof, but they are remarkable evidence, and many people's lives have been changed after viewing them.

However, those who return from healing pilgrimages are not unanimous in their endorsement of the phenomenon or the storied God-like qualities of the healers. Many persons return disillusioned and bitter, feeling that they were fleeced by an extremely clever confidence game. The proportion of those returning satisfied to those returning disillusioned is roughly seven to three. Few people return noncommittal; a former patient usually is either on the healer's bandwagon or after his scalp.

Behind every such legend there is at least an iota of truth. Are all the thousands of cures reported purely psychological? Are all those persons who accept the phenomenon on the basis of their own experience irrational?

Take the case of Joy Hunt, an intelligent, practical, well-to-do suburbanite. Life was an exciting, wonderful business for her and her yachtsman husband until she began having headaches, corresponding to fuzzy vision in her right eye. Eye specialists at Northwestern University diagnosed a malignant tumor affecting the retina of the right eye, and they recommended that the eye be removed.

Joy was crushed by the news. She was determined to get the best possible care, so she and her husband flew to New York for diagnosis by a leading eye cancer specialist. It was September, 1970, when the doctor confirmed the earlier diagnosis— cancer.

"It's an incredible thing to hear," Joy said. "I was shocked out of my wits. They wanted to remove my eye because the cancer might endanger my life. I told Bill I would do anything, even go to that healer or whatever in the Philippines, but *nobody* was taking my eye out."

It's odd that Joy had remembered that there was such a thing as a Filipino healer. It had been more than a year since her mother had called and told her a fantastic tale about psychic surgery. Joy had scoffed at the story, and her mother never mentioned the subject again.

"I was an intellectual snob then, and when mother told me about Tony Agpaoa I wasn't at all interested. It sounded freaky to me."

However, after sweating through five and a half hours of tests on her eye, Joy decided to find out about the Filipino healers. She looked up Greta Deal, of Chicago's North Side. Descriptions of brain surgery performed on Greta Deal by Tony Agpaoa propel many people to investigate the phenomenon. Before her psychic surgery Greta had been paralyzed by a severe stroke. The Hunts visited others who had been helped by the phenomenal surgery and viewed several films. Those who told their stories had nothing to gain by convincing the Hunts.

"All the people we talked to were sincere and really wanted to help me. Bill finally said, 'I still don't believe it, but I want you to have any possible chance there might be, so we'll go. Besides, I want to see this for myself.' Today Bill isn't on the bandwagon, but he believes without getting carried away."

In the Philippines Joy visited Juan Blanche, a healer lesser known to Americans than Agpaoa but more highly respected by native Filipinos.

"I was terrified. I had to lie down on a dirty wooden table. The room was filthy, and there was a big bug crawling on the wall.

"I felt his fingers inside my eye socket. He used his forefinger and thumb to squeeze my eyeball. There wasn't any pain, then all of a sudden this little thing popped out of the corner of my eye."

Joy also visited Eleuterio Terte, an aged healer who is credited with founding the Espiritistas Union, the religious body to which most healers belong.

"Terte looks like an ancient Hindu more than he does a Filipino. It is said he has the third eye, so I wanted him to check me out. My vision was still fuzzy, so I wasn't positive about Blanche's effectiveness. Terte said he saw something, and he said, 'Hold your eye open.' I held it open, and he pointed his right forefinger at me from what appeared to be about seven inches away. Suddenly I felt an electrical shock, and my eye started watering. I wasn't certain what had happened, so I asked Bill if he had stuck his finger in my eye. Bill shook his head and said, 'No, he just pointed at your eye.' "

The highly qualified medical opinion back in the United States was that Joy Hunt's retina tumor had "regressed."

"In all his years of experience my doctor has encountered only four other natural regressions," said Joy. "Such a thing is so uncommon he's written papers about them. Of course I didn't tell him about the Philippines trip; how could I tell a man of his stature such a thing?"

If it was a natural regression, despite the astronomical odds against it, Joy experienced another healing that leaves no room for doubt.

"When I was young, I had scarlet fever and my right ear drum was badly scarred. Blanche asked me about the ear every time I saw him, and finally on my last visit he grabbed me by the shoulders and pointed to my ear. I would have refused had I known what was coming. He broke off several match sticks, placed them in my ear, and smacked them sharply with the flat of his hand. There was a flash of intense pain; then he pulled the matches out of my ear. The frayed match ends were covered with a black goop. My ear ached, and a watery solution ran lightly out of it for two days. Then it stopped and I felt fine. I had a specialist check it when we were home and he said, 'That's the weirdest thing I've ever seen. You have a perfect hole in your ear drum.' I said I felt fine, so he shrugged and said the rest of my ear looked normal. But it *hadn't* looked right since I was six years old."

This experience had a profound effect on Joy Hunt's life: "Everything I'd ever known and judged to be true was no longer absolute," she said.

She returned to the Philippines in 1971 and studied with Agpaoa for several months. During her tenure she saw a number of incredible operations, including one on a man who had a retina cancer precisely like hers. "Tony literally took the eye out of the socket, turned it around, and had me take the tumor off with forceps."

Joy, like many others who have experienced this form of healing, stresses that "the soul healing one gets from this is more important than the physical healing." An opinion with which, though miles apart from Joy Hunt on the social spectrum, Irene Przybycien of Chicago agrees.

Irene's uncluttered description of her psychic surgery opens this book. She's fifty years old now and in excellent health. She is also filled with contentment and charity toward others despite working in the hectic will-call department of a major department store.

"I used to hate the noise and the impatient people, but I truly love people now. Tony had a way of bringing a curtain of serenity down around everyone, and after experiencing his healing a person just has to come back feeling good about mankind."

Irene had a number of maladies corrected by Agpaoa during a visit in January, 1971.

"My esophagus somehow plugged up, and I couldn't eat. Things were pretty desperate. Even soups came back up. My doctor thought at first that it was a gall bladder problem; then he thought it was nerves. Finally he called in some other doctors, and they thought it could be an ulcer or maybe a tumor of some kind. They wanted me in a hospital so that they could open me up and see what was wrong. I would have been laid up for weeks, and it would have cost a bundle. I chose to go to the Philippines instead.

"I had all kinds of things wrong with me, but Tony knew about them just by looking me over. He took care of everything, too. First he took a chunk of meaty stuff about two inches long out of my chest. He said I could eat what I wanted after that, and he was right. I ate anything and everything without a bit of trouble. He also removed some massed tissue from around my ovaries, which pressed against my hip, making it hard for me to walk. He even knew I had bothersome things behind my eyes, kind of like pieces of gravel hurting me. I felt his finger in behind my eyes, and he removed some burrlike things. I don't know what they were, but I haven't had any pain there since."

One's first thought about Irene's testimony might be that her level of education detracts from her credibility. Irene admits that she is no intellectual, but she demonstrates uncommonly good sense. Her statement on the matter handles the problem of her credibility quite well:

"Sure, doctors are great, and we need them. But they don't know everything. If you go to a doctor, you have to tell him what's wrong before he can do anything. So if I'm smart enough to know what's wrong in order to tell my doctor, how come I'm not smart enough to know what's wrong when I go to the Philippines?"

She's also quick to point out that Agpaoa didn't ask her what was wrong; he figured it out for himself and fixed it.

Carroll English, a schoolteacher, tells a remarkable story and shows color slides to support her claims. Carroll's report was the first of a long line of firsthand accounts that I gathered during the past four years.

For fifteen years Carroll endured symptoms of a chronic spastic colon; then in 1966 the condition became acute. Her digestive and metabolic systems degenerated to the point at which she was not assimilating protein.

"I was allergic to most foods. I was always fatigued, and headaches were practically continual. I thought it was all psychosomatic, and perhaps that was the original cause, but two doctors diagnosed my ailments as physical."

Urinalysis and a scratch test verified her allergies. But her condition baffled her doctors, and she was sent to an allergy specialist.

In addition Carroll had a painful leg-hip problem, and she consulted an osteopath. X rays showed the right leg to be an inch shorter than the left, so a lift was constructed for her shoe. Carroll was in misery. Her doctors seemed powerless; years of consultation and treatment had wrought no improvement.

"I was really a wreck. I had all kinds of stress symptoms and nerve fatigue, and my lungs were unable to absorb very much oxygen. I was on the brink of giving up when I heard about Dr. Tony and decided I had nothing to lose by visiting the Philippines."

Carroll borrowed money to make the trip in June, 1968. She had outlined her symptoms in a letter to Tony, so she cannot be certain how much of his ultimate diagnosis was psychic and how much was obtained from normal information. In any case, just before her operation Tony asked her to describe her symptoms, and she did.

"I asked Tony why he was asking me about my problem because I had heard he diagnosed without being told. He replied that he wanted me to talk in order to relieve the tension and apprehension I was feeling toward submitting to this curious form of surgery."

Carroll still can describe her operations in detail and will illustrate with excellent quality slides whenever someone requests it.

"Tony had me lie down on a table that was covered with plastic. He asked me to bend my knees, and I did. While he observed whatever it was he was observing within me, his assistants rubbed the healer's oil on my brow. It made my eyes smart a little because it's strong like a liniment.

"I felt the right side of me slice open and Tony's hand press in. He asked me if it hurt. I told him it hurt a little. I was fully aware of everything he was doing, but I could tolerate it. The pain was not acute. Tony then asked if I wanted to watch with a mirror. I said yes; then I grew apprehensive and said no. He

then insisted, and he had Rosita [his assistant] show me the
opening in the mirror. He demanded that I watch. As I looked
at the opening in my body, Tony pointed out each organ that
could be seen. I didn't relish sitting there with my abdomen
hanging open, and I wished he'd hurry along. However, Tony
was in no hurry. He obligingly held the incision wide open as
long as necessary for Rosita to take pictures and for the throng
of curious onlookers to peer inside of me."

In this case Tony removed the "diseased tissue" from the
area of her colon with an instrument other than his hands, and
still there was no acute pain or scar tissue.

"Tony used surgical scissors to clip away some colon tissue,
and he didn't even look at what he was doing. He looked around
the room and in my face all the while. When he held the severed
tissue up for me to see, it looked like a piece of bloody chicken
entrail. I'm not implying that it was chicken; it's just that I've
seen chicken entrail before and can draw a comparison.

"Tony had Rosita put the camera down and hold the mirror
so that I could watch the closing. His hands worked furiously
inside me—kneading my flesh as if it were dough. My blood
bubbled and gurgled and sloshed down my side. I felt queasy.
Then he lifted a large piece of blood-soaked cotton out from
inside my wound. How he put it in there without my knowing it
is a mystery, but then the whole thing's a mystery. He held his
thumb and forefinger at the ends of the incision; then he suddenly pulled his hand away and everything snapped back together."

Carroll's flesh closed instantly, and there is no evidence that
an opening ever existed. She hardly had time to catch her breath
when Tony commanded her to roll over for another operation
on her back.

"He dug right into the base of my spine and removed a piece
of cartilage; then he showed it to me by holding it over my
shoulder with the scissors. It looked like a piece of bloody fat."

Carroll sustained some postoperative trauma and some of
the blood stained her clothing, but otherwise she felt immediate
improvement. Tony told her she could now eat anything, but he

advised her to maintain a balanced diet. He added that her physical problems were real but that they had been caused by her mind. "Think better thoughts," he said.

Almost as an afterthought, she was instructed to remove the lift from her shoe. The right leg was no longer shorter than the left.

Carroll returned home with renewed health and vitality. As of this writing she is still in excellent health.

Carroll's testimony and slides were my first serving of "white crow." William James pointed out that it only takes one white crow to prove that not all crows are black. One concrete case is all that is needed to make psychic surgery possible.

Carroll English learned of the Filipino healer from Rosita Rodriguez, Tony's missionary in Chicago. Rosita visited Tony to study at the same time Carroll made the trip. She is an ordained minister in Agpaoa's church—the Philippine Church of Science and Revelation. She is also Agpaoa's principal representative in the United States. Rosita and the Chicago mission have been largely responsible for Tony's substantial Chicago following.

In November, 1968, Agpaoa visited the United States, and Rosita brought him to the home of some very close friends, where he gave an impromptu demonstration of his healing powers. He performed minor surgery on Sandy Cysewski, and the operation was witnessed at close range by several persons, including Carroll English and Sandy's husband at that time, David Cysewski. Accounts of this event were my second helping of white crow.

Sandy had a small fatty cyst, about the size of a cherry, above her left breast. It wasn't necessarily a threat to her health, but it was such a nuisance that it bothered her a great deal. David Cysewski, who watched intently from only a foot away, gave this account:

"Tony worked very slowly; there was no quick movement of his hands; nothing that smacked of sleight of hand. He took a long time, and I thought he was working hard. When he squeezed the cyst out, he left the wound open to allow it to drain. As far as I know, Sandy still has a small opening there."

Rosita, who is a qualified surgical assistant, explained the reason for leaving the incision open:

"There was infection under the cyst. This isn't common, but Sandy must have irritated it. The last time I saw her, more than a year after the operation, she still had a tiny hole in her skin and a depression where the hard cyst had been."

Agpaoa impressed everyone present. He had performed what he termed a "simple" operation on a woman he had never seen before. He worked in a strange home, in a strange land, before the questioning eyes of many strangers.

The hostess made this observation of Tony:

"He seemed to have a quiet wisdom. He was gentle and unpretentious. I felt he was succumbing to the pressure and demands of others, and I'm not certain he liked what he was doing. He certainly wasn't devious. He was very straightforward, almost childlike."

After viewing several home movies and interviewing a number of persons with documented testimony upholding psychic surgery, I became convinced that the phenomenon was genuine. Unexplained, but genuine.

As I continued my research, I reached a point at which I accepted his storied abilities and indeed defended him against detractors. Whenever someone labeled Agpaoa a fake or a charlatan, I demanded specifics. For the most part those persons who called Agpaoa a fraud had no more proof in a clinical sense than I had to defend him as a wonder worker.

Rosita told me some wonderful tales about Tony. She said that Tony first discovered he had healing power when he was seven years old. A playmate had fallen from a tree and gashed himself badly. As the villagers were carrying the youngster to another town, where a doctor lived, Tony fretted about the bleeding and tried to stop it with a piece of cloth. When he put his hands on the wound, it suddenly stopped bleeding and began to heal. The peasants fell on their knees and prayed. To them Tony's actions were a miracle from God.

Rosita met Tony in 1966, when he visited the United States for the first time. She believes that a chiropractor was responsible for Tony's first visit. (The medical practitioners who showed early interest in psychic surgery were chiropractors.) Tony lectured at that time, and Rosita met him after his talk. Agpaoa has since visited the United States three times, the last time in the fall of 1968, which turned into a personal disaster for him. He was arrested and charged with fraud in November. He waited to be brought to trial in Detroit for nearly four months before he finally jumped bail ($25,000) and returned to his home and family. This act made him a fugitive in the United States, and the case is still pending in Detroit federal court.

Rosita described an incident in which twenty-three ophthalmologists from Los Angeles went to the Philippines with three blind patients, glaucoma and cataracts cases. Agpaoa's barehanded surgery, performed before the unbelieving eyes of the medical doctors, cured all three. The ophthalmologists allegedly wrote of the cases to their association and urged further study. They were advised to forget it.

Rosita told a story about Tony's visit to a gathering of Oriental mystics, fakirs, swamis, and other miracle workers. Some fabulous phenomena were displayed at this convention, held in Japan, but when it was Tony's turn to perform, he refused, saying that he didn't demonstrate for the sake of show. One of the delegates challenged him, saying that Tony's refusal indicated that he was a fraud. The man then cajoled Tony into a quick performance by defying him to pull a tooth. This fellow pointed to one of his own front teeth and challenged Tony to prove he was a miracle surgeon. Tony reached out, pulled the tooth, and handed it to the astonished challenger.

The story may be colorful fiction, but the extraction of teeth by psychic surgery is well documented. We have an expression about pulling teeth that indicates it is no easy task to extract them, yet Agpaoa and other healers reach into mouths and remove teeth with amazing ease—using only their fingers.

In his book *Wonder Healers of the Philippines* veteran researcher Harold Sherman describes how Dr. Seymour S.

Wanderman, of New York, checked the teeth in a patient's mouth before Tony extracted them. The teeth were firmly embedded, but Agpaoa pulled them as if they were rooted in butter.

Ron Ormond, whose article "Bloodless Surgery by the Strange Healer of San Fabian," in *Fate* magazine, April, 1960, focused attention on the phenomenon for the first time, described a tooth extraction he witnessed as follows:

"Later, one of Terte's assistants and followers, twenty-year-old Juan Enbarnal, took over to extract some teeth. The first man upon whom he 'operated' was in obvious pain from a visibly abscessed molar. Yet the patient seemed to feel no pain as Enbarnal's fingers touched the tooth.

"McGill [co-author Ormond McGill] was at the healer's elbow, watching every move, while I shot over his shoulder with the camera. There was an audible clicking sound as the tooth was released from the jawbone, yet the young man's thumb and forefinger seemed to touch it only gently. Both of us examined the tooth, new and raw, then examined the gaping hole where the tooth had been. But there was no blood. And the infected area had disappeared. . . ."

All this testimony is not, of course, concrete proof in a clinical sense. During 1970-1971 my wife and I interviewed more than a hundred persons who had experienced psychic surgery, and we watched many home movies of the phenomenon. We heard from individuals who ranked Tony Agpaoa alongside Jesus Christ and from others who ranked him alongside Judas Iscariot. Then we met Ralph and Sonia Pope, who presented a case history that appeared to offer the "concrete proof."

Ralph, Sonia, and Sonia's mother, Mrs. Raymond Steinberg made the healing pilgrimage to Tony's Baguio City home in October, 1970. Ralph, an incorrigible golfer, was skeptical, but Sonia promised him many rounds over Oriental fairways if he consented to make the trip.

Like Carroll English, Sonia Pope had a number of ailments for which she had been treated unsuccessfully by various specialists for a number of years. Sonia underwent several psychic operations, and after seeing them Ralph's attitude changed. He consented to some surgery on himself. One of Ralph's problems was severe hemorrhoids, and Tony operated, easing the pain instantly. If any psychic surgery is convincing, it is the handling of this painful problem. It is inconceivable that Agpaoa or any healer can ram his hand into another man's painful rectum without possessing some kind of phenomenal ability.

For the benefit of their home movies, Sonia and Ralph removed the polyps from each other's noses after Tony prepared the way with his bare-handed surgery. It seemed that their trip was more a lark than a pilgrimage to overcome misery and illness. They returned to the States singing the praises of Tony and psychic surgery. And, in the case of Mrs. Steinberg, they brought back "positive proof."

On the Saturday following Thanksgiving, 1969, Mrs. Steinberg was in an auto accident. Her husband swerved to avoid another car, the pavement was icy and slick, and their car skidded into a culvert. The door smashed in on Mrs. Steinberg's right side, and the door handle broke her hip. Her family doctor and a specialist from Sheboygan braced her broken bone with a large metal pin, a plate, and five screws. For nearly a year after this surgery Mrs. Steinberg experienced pain in her hip and leg. She was unable to walk without assistance, and she could not sleep on her right side.

In Baguio City Mrs. Steinberg had a huge piece of tissue removed, which Tony identified as an ulcer. Then, almost as an afterthought, Sonia wondered whether Tony might be able to do anything for her mother's hip pains.

"We explained to Tony that it didn't really matter. If he couldn't do it, we would understand. We didn't pressure him in any way, but he said he would take care of it."

On October 28, 1970, Agpaoa made a major production out of performing the hip operation on Mrs. Steinberg. He told Ralph and Sonia that no photographs would be allowed. He seemed unusually somber as he worked (he is usually quite jovial when operating), and he kept his hands hidden beneath a towel. The Popes and Mrs. Steinberg had already seen enough to be convinced of his phenomenal ability, so they didn't question the unusual proceedings.

Tony held a piece of metal and some screws up for Mrs. Steinberg to see, explaining he had removed them from her hip bone.

"Tony told us that he removed four of the five pins that held the plate and the flat metal plate itself. He said he had used some plastic material to fill the holes in her bone."

Agpaoa then did something unusual. He bandaged Mrs. Steinberg's hip with layers of tape and told her to rest in bed all day. He did not explain the need for the bandage. After the day of recuperation Mrs. Steinberg was able to walk without pain.

By May, 1971, the Popes had shown their movies and told their story to hundreds of others. Ralph had shown his films at several Kiwanis luncheons. They found themselves confronted with heavy, insulting skepticism. Sonia, incensed by skeptical reactions from persons who had never heard of psychic surgery, suggested that her mother have x rays taken to prove that the metal plate and four screws had been removed. X ray proof before and after bare-handed surgery should silence the critics once and for all.

Mrs. Steinberg did not wish to antagonize her family doctor, so she went to a neighboring city to a clinic for x rays. The doctor there knew nothing of her problem or her trip to the Philippines. When he observed the large pin in her hip, he asked about her pain. During the conversation he said pointedly, "Well, there is a pin in your hip." Since he failed to mention the plate and screws, and since she was convinced that they had been removed, Mrs. Steinberg did not question the doctor further. She accepted his statement as documentation that the psychic surgery indeed removed the metal objects.

"I even danced on New Year's Eve," she told my wife and me in the spring of 1972 while we were in Two Rivers to see both doctors in order to confirm the x ray proof. I had encountered some inconsistency regarding the phenomenon and its practitioners, so my faith needed bolstering.

We compared an old x ray to the post-Philippine x ray. There was no apparent difference.

I told Mrs. Steinberg that I could see no difference between the x rays. She immediately called the doctor and the mystery of the x rays was solved. There was *no* change.

Ralph and Sonia, who told me in 1971, "There isn't a selfish bone in Tony's body; he's a prince of a guy," were now telling me, "Tony's a big phony—he really pulled a fast one on us, just to get an extra $300 out of us."

Mrs. Steinberg has since had the metal objects removed by orthodox surgery. Sonia now feels that Tony's other operations availed her little if any relief. The only thing they don't doubt is that Tony fixed Ralph's hemorrhoids.

Money paid to Tony Agpaoa is at the crux of the controversy. But does money really have anything to do with the body-opening phenomenon? Does one lie—or a dozen frauds—condemn the entire phenomenon of psychic surgery to the quack heap? Do the fraudulent cases cancel out the real ones?

If parapsychology and modern science are incompatible, why not reject parapsychology? We know that the alternate hypothesis, that some men lie or deceive themselves, fits quite well within the framework of science. The choice is between believing in something "truly revolutionary" and "radically contradictory to contemporary thought" and believing in the occurrence of fraud and self-delusion. Which is more reasonable?

Dr. George R. Price
Science magazine, 1955

2 A Fraud, a Fake, a Fugitive

"TONY AGPAOA is 100 percent fraud, and I can prove it."

William J. Monaghan, a staff investigator for the American Medical Association, was speaking over the phone. He had been informed that I had advocated psychic surgery during a television interview, and he had called to let me know, in no uncertain terms, the official position concerning the phenomenon.

Shortly after the telephone conversation I made an appointment to see Monaghan in his office at AMA headquarters. I wanted to see his "proof" that Agpaoa was 100 percent fraud.

While waiting for Monaghan to meet me at the security guard's desk, I glanced around the busy office building and mused about the tremendous responsibility the employees of this organization carry. And when I saw Bill Monaghan, I saw a dedicated employee. He is tall, hawkish, and assured, precisely what one would expect in a man who is responsible for many quackery and medical hoax investigations.

Looking back, I'm not certain exactly what I anticipated he would show me as proof. Perhaps I expected to see movies that I had heard rumors about. A young woman had told me that psychic surgery was a lot of bunk, and she knew what she was talking about because her older brother was in medical school, and they had shown him movies disclosing the Filipino fakery. So I was surprised when Monaghan proceeded to bring a huge pile of old newspaper clippings from his files, which, he explained, were his proof.

"I thought you had proof to show me," I protested. "These clippings aren't proof. For every story that alleges fraud, I can dig up two that claim he's a miracle worker."

"Read those," he said, pointing with his finger to the clippings, mostly from the *Detroit Free Press* concerning a highly publicized pilgrimage from that city in 1967. "Read them closely, and you will see he's nothing but a fraud."

I had already seen these clippings and many more during my previous two years of research. I tried to reason with Monaghan; I explained that allegations printed in newspapers were not acceptable as proof of anything by anybody. "If I presented you with a pile of newspaper clippings saying that Agpaoa was a proven miracle healer, would you consider them proof?" I asked.

"Of course not," was Monaghan's reply.

"Then how can you expect me to accept these clippings as proof that he's a fraud?"

"Well, read them and see what they say," he insisted. "Look at this one. A man had blood on his clothing analyzed, and it turned out to be chicken blood. What do you say to that?"

To my amazement Monaghan was serious, and his mind was made up. I tried getting through to him anyway.

"This story"—I held up the clipping—"makes some unsubstantiated allegations and proves nothing. The laboratory that analyzed the bloodstains is not named; besides, thorough analysis of any biochemical materials usually requires two or more independent laboratory tests—you ought to know that. This news story you call proof is nothing but a news story."

Unabashed, Monaghan pulled a letter out of his drawer. It was written by Harold Sherman, the researcher and author who personally studied Agpaoa and other healers before writing *Wonder Healers of the Philippines,* in 1967. Sherman is a veteran researcher of phenomena, one of the most esteemed in the world, and his book was thoroughly objective. His letter essentially informed the AMA in general and Monaghan in particular that Harold Sherman did not consider the AMA to be openminded enough for him to take the time and effort to explain fully what he observed in the Philippines.

I read the letter, shook my head, and wondered why Monaghan didn't have a copy of Sherman's book among his pile of "proof" clippings. I asked about Sherman's book; then I held the letter up and added:

"This is more of a slap in the face for you than proof of anything."

"It shows you the kind of people we are forced to deal with in this matter. Now here's a letter from a highly qualified person. Read it . . . especially this part . . ." He pointed to a paragraph on the second page of the lengthy letter.

The letter was from Dr. Ian Stevenson, of the University of Virginia Medical School, one of the world's leading authorities on the psychology of unexplained phenomena. Dr. Stevenson has studied reincarnation thoroughly and his book *Twenty Cases Suggestive of Reincarnation* is a masterful presentation. I wondered to myself if Monaghan knew that his highly qualified letter writer had written a book about reincarnation.

Dr. Stevenson had visited the Philippines to investigate psychic surgery claims. His letter to Monaghan explained that he had been unable to see Agpaoa because the healer avoided their meeting. Tony hedged on the meeting with the scientist "because of a typhoon," but there were no typhoons in the area at that time, Dr. Stevenson said.

Dr. Stevenson's letter described an operation performed by Terte in which the healer claimed to have removed gallstones. Dr. Stevenson was unable to explain what he observed, but he was allowed to keep the stones for analysis. He had the stones analyzed; one report considered them to be organic stone and therefore genuine. The other report labeled them limestone. It was the part about the limestone to which Monaghan had pointed.

I surveyed Monaghan's pile of clippings and letters with a shrug and said: "This isn't proof; in fact, it isn't even good evidence. I've got better evidence of some fakery than anything you've shown me here. How can you claim to have proof on this basis? Haven't you or the AMA studied this matter?"

"The burden of proof doesn't rest with us, Mr. Valentine. The burden of proof is on those who make the claims. If you believe this quackery is genuine, then it's up to you to bring in positive proof."

I was dumbfounded.

"You're telling me that if I accept psychic surgery as valid, it's up to me to prove it to you. Until I do, you refuse to in-

vestigate but will continue putting out unstudied propaganda—
like that garbage in *Time* magazine?"

My mention of *Time* brought a raised eyebrow from Monaghan. "Frankly, I'm surprised you don't have those articles in
your file."

"I do," he replied.

Time quoted Dr. Gerald D. Dorman, AMA president 1968-
1969, as saying that Agpaoa "is a former sleight-of-hand artist."
That statement is unsubstantiated by Tony's history. In the same
article Dorman lampooned the closing of the wounds without
leaving a scar by saying: "It's perfectly logical, since his laying on of hands actually involves no opening." Dr. Dorman
was making strong statements without a thorough investigation
to back them up.

"Do you really believe in this psychic surgery?" Monaghan
asked incredulously.

"The phenomenon has been demonstrated conclusively, and
I've studied it for a number of years."

"Have you seen it?"

I decided to lie. I had not yet made a trip to the Philippines.
"Yes, I've seen it. Right here in Chicago."

"Well, that's still purely subjective, isn't it?" he snapped.

I was at a loss for a retort. To me Monaghan's attitude was
unreal. Suddenly he changed his demeanor, and he became the
investigator: "You say you saw him in Chicago. Would you
care to elaborate, tell me the details of what took place?"

I realized why he was suddenly so interested. "Why? So
you can charge him with practicing medicine without a license?"

"That's right," he said, without so much as a wince.

"Don't you find that just a bit inconsistent?" I asked.

"How do you mean?"

"Well, if Agpaoa is a 100 percent fraud, as you claim to have
proved, then even if I testify to the details of an operation here
in Chicago, you can't charge him with practicing medicine
illegally without admitting that he's *practicing medicine*. He's
either a fake or a surgeon, Mr. Monaghan."

Monaghan was impervious to my response. He looked me in the eye and said: "Tony Agpaoa is a fugitive from justice. Did you know that?"

"Yes, I know all about the case."

"Doesn't that make any difference to you?" he asked.

"I'm only interested in whether the phenomenon has ever been genuine; one time is all that's necessary. It doesn't matter who performed it or how much money he made or whether his mother wore army boots—all that matters is the fact such a thing can be possible. Not consistent—*possible*. Once this is is established, we can go into other ramifications. I feel it has been so established. You do not."

The interview was ended. In fairness to Monaghan's work, and to the medical profession, everyone should realize that innumerable forms of quackery exist, and hundreds of clever, unscrupulous persons prey on the gullibility of the sick and the desperate. It's Monaghan's job to curb quackery to the best of his ability—and that's a full-time chore. For example, during 1970-1971 it was reported that a Filipino man and woman were posing as Tony and Lucy Agpaoa in order to capitalize on the healer's fame. They were performing magnetic healings in various cities around the United States, and ailing suckers donated considerable cash for the bogus treatments only to learn that they had been swindled.

A 1972 survey by *Life* magazine stressed that we Americans consider our medical care to be good. In the main, doctors are quality professionals and quality people.

Generally, physicians deserve their high esteem. However, my session with Monaghan and the abortive attempt to discuss psychic surgery on a "scientific" basis reminded me of the words spoken by a scientist friend who disputed medical orthodoxy:

"The medical profession is undeservedly pompous when biological sciences are considered. By their own testimony in courts of law, medical doctors are not scientists but practitioners of an art. Yet when it comes to legislation, our law-making bodies accept the *opinions* of these practitioners as scientific fact, despite many instances where fact contradicts opinion."

Charges of fraud and commercialism have clouded the scientific issue of psychic surgery. Though the charges are not relevant to the phenomenon, researchers are forced to deal with these allegations objectively.

It's true that Agpaoa is a fugitive from justice. He was indicted by a Federal Grand Jury in Detroit on December 19, 1968, following his arrest in San Francisco a month earlier. He was charged with fraud in foreign commerce, and his trial date was set for January 23, 1969. The first trial date was adjourned till January 30 because the defendant failed to appear. On January 30 the case was "called by proclamation" because Agpaoa was in the Philippines, having jumped bail. As of this writing the case has been reassigned to Judge Fred Case in the United States District Court in Detroit, Michigan. Agpaoa's attorneys moved to have the case dismissed in 1972, but their motion was denied. The case is still pending. Tony has been urged to return and clear himself, but there is fear he will not get a chance to answer the original charge because of the fugitive charges.

Rumor and misinformation surround the arrest of the Filipino healer. I learned the facts from George Newman, the assistant United States Attorney in Detroit, who was the prosecutor.

Newman claims full and direct responsibility for the investigation and prosecution by federal authorities:

"I first became aware of this man and his claims when news stories told of sick people mortgaging their homes to make the pilgrimage. I was personally outraged. There was no way in hell he could be legitimate. Then when another big group was publicly planning to go, there was widespread community outrage. [He refers to the October, 1967, chartered flight of 109 Americans and 2 Canadians, which departed from Windsor, Ontario.] The county district attorney was powerless to answer complaints. Then when money was transferred from a bank in Warren, Michigan, to a Canadian bank [more than $70,000 to pay for the chartered flight], I had jurisdiction to investigate. I was out to get him."

Newman told me that since United States attorneys do not have direct investigative staffs, they must rely upon other federal agencies. "I conferred with Bob Grace [then the United States Attorney], and we asked the FBI to investigate. We obtained a warrant, and when Agpaoa returned to the United States in November of 1968, the FBI arrested him in San Francisco."

Newman judged that Agpaoa was claiming the impossible and was perpetrating a cruel hoax by building false hopes in desperately ill persons. He believed it was his duty to protect the gullible. Medical opinion supported him, and additional evidence was gathered when many of the pilgrims from the 1967 trip returned bitterly disappointed.

"I interviewed about fifteen victims of the fraud," Newman explained, "and I noted a recurrent theme. Nearly all the victims had high expectations, serious illness, and financial difficulties.

"Yes, you can say I was out to get him," he added.

Newman was not alone in his quest to squelch Tony's bids for American popularity. Patrick Ruddy, on the staff of the Illinois Attorney General, boasted that in the summer of 1967 he and agents from the United States Post Office "ran Dr. Tony out of Chicago, where he was drumming up business for his practice in the Philippines."

When Ruddy and the postal agents apprehended Tony, Curtis and Mary Fuller, the founders of *Fate* magazine, were among the group with the healer. Mary Fuller recalls: "We went to the Philippine consulate office with Tony, and I was handed a paper bag to hold for him. It was filled with money. I have no idea how much was in there, but it was filled with bills."

It isn't known if that bag of money was part of the collections for the Detroit pilgrimage or if it was intended for Tony's church. However, money and commercialism seem to be linked to the phenomenon whenever Tony Agpaoa's abilities are discussed.

Detroit's prominent role in the saga of psychic surgery is mainly due to the remarkable recovery of one man: Joseph Ruffner, a steel worker from Wyandotte, Michigan, whose "cure" from a crippling back injury triggered an avalanche of favorable publicity for Agpaoa.

Joe Ruffner fell thirty-two feet from the top of a trimming machine in August, 1956. He broke his back and suffered several years of excruciating pain. Numerous operations and tests by specialists failed to bring relief.

"I thought about suicide. I begged my wife to leave me, and at night, in bed, I'd cry," he reported.

Four years after his fall he was declared handicapped and began receiving Social Security. In 1965 he heard about Agpaoa and psychic surgery, but he considered the idea "crackpot." In 1966 he read an article about Agpaoa's miracle medicine, and he complained to his wife: "This is terrible. Why should people's hopes be raised by such promises?"

His wife suggested he write the Filipino healer just to see what would happen. He wrote explaining his situation and his lack of money, but he did not expect to hear from Agpaoa. A return letter from Tony told him he needed no money, that if it were God's will, he would get to the Philippines and be cured.

Friends and benefactors Ruffner never dreamed existed came forward with contributions, and soon he was determined to go to the Philippines. Had not Tony's letter told him that the means to make the trip would be provided by God? But doubts were raised about traveling to a strange land in a crippled condition. Then the doubts were dispelled. A Filipino man in the United States Navy unexpectedly called for Ruffner's notary service. The sailor's mother lived in Baguio City, and he told Ruffner that if the American visited Baguio, he could stay at his mother's home. Ruffner regarded the sailor's coincidental visit as a good omen. He flew to the Philippines.

On November 3, 1966, alone and barely able to move about on crutches, Ruffner arrived in Manila. A policeman offered to drive him to the healer for three hundred pesos. He was driven around for a long time, returned to his hotel, and told, "The healer you seek cannot be found."

The next day Ruffner rode a native bus from Manila to Baguio; a grinding, hot, hectic 160 miles. When he reached his destination, he had no idea of how to find Agpaoa, but the bus driver extended hospitality, refused all payment, and helped him find Agpaoa's home the next morning. He was told to return for healing that afternoon.

Checking into a hotel, Ruffner encountered a man who was loudly proclaiming Agpaoa a fake. Ruffner ignored the man's protestations and returned to the healer's home in the afternoon. Tony was operating in a bedroom as Ruffner arrived. Several Americans, part of a tour guided by Dr. Bernard Jensen, a California chiropractor, were in Agpaoa's home. Among the more interested viewers were a medical doctor from UCLA and the widow of a physician whose story equals that of Joe Ruffner. Ruffner hobbled into the bedroom, hauled up his shirt, lowered his trousers, and awaited the strange surgery as strangers crowded closer to see or to take pictures.

"I was scared, but I didn't feel any pain. I saw him cut into me with his bare hands and dig something out. I saw it open, I saw it close, and I saw blood. A guy who said he was a doctor asked me if he could put his hand into my wound. I said it was okay by me if it was clean. He put his hand in, and I could feel it. When he drew it out, it was covered with blood. Then Tony took his hands out, and the wound was instantly healed. He said to me, 'Get up and walk.' I didn't think I could—you know, after surgery and all—but I did. Tony then said, 'Go home and rest,' but some doctors examined me first, and it seemed they couldn't believe what they had seen."

Ruffner returned to his hotel—walking without pain and without his crutches for the first time in nearly a decade. His spirits soared. When he spied the man who had proclaimed the healer a fake, he strode up, put his arms around the man, and hoisted him off the ground in a dramatic demonstration of his healing. The man, whom Ruffner did not know, was television personality Joe Pyne.

Ruffner happily announced his healing, and the press delighted in helping him tell the story. It was fascinating and thoroughly documented testimony. The many specialists who had been treating Ruffner were asked to explain. The consensus of medical opinion was: "His ailment must have been in his head."

"If that's true," Ruffner challenged, "why the hell have you guys worked on my back all this time?"

Ruffner's problems were magnified when later x rays revealed that his bones were still broken. He should not have been able to walk, despite the obvious fact that he was walking and picking people up to prove his back was strong. Agpaoa had not mended his bones, but he had removed the pain. Was this fraud? Was it hypnosis or powerful psychology at work? It didn't matter to Ruffner; what counted was his experience. He took others to the Philippines and brought them back "cured"—to the further delight of the press. Ruffner's obtrusive work on Tony's behalf caused George Newman to notice the blatant claims; it was Ruffner who organized the strangest of healing pilgrimages in the fall of 1967.

Philippine Medical Association officials, pressured by the AMA, had Agpaoa under surveillance when the planeload of desperate but hopeful people arrived in the islands.

Mary Fuller, editor of *Fate* magazine, wrote a descriptive account of the 1967 pilgrimage. I have not been able to improve on her reporting, so I include her article in its entirety. This story appeared in the March, 1968, issue of *Fate* under the title: "Story of a Pilgrimage; 111 in Search of a Miracle."

At night the stars hang low over the beach, and the breeze is warm and soft from the South China Sea. Nevertheless, the Cresta Ola resort hotel, in a rural region on the west side of the Philippines' largest island where long distance telephones do not operate around the clock, seems a strange, unnerving place to wait for the blessing of faith. The hotel

backs up to the sea, dotted with the long outrigger boats of local fisher-
men. Every morning an eight-year-old boy leads two huge broad-
horned carabaos, domesticated Philippine water buffalo, along the
nearby bumpy rock and mud road, past the muddy canal and the rice
field to put them out to graze. Beyond are the mountains.

On one lovely evening last fall the mellow voice of a woman was
heard singing, "If happy little bluebirds fly beyond the rainbow, why,
oh why, can't I?"

The woman sat in a wheelchair cradling a microphone while a
Filipino combo accompanied her with slow background music. Connie
Brubaugh, 39, mother of two, had come all the way from Cass Lake,
Michigan. That night, dressed in pale yellow with a white flower in her
dark hair and gold sandals on her feet, she sang for a long time. Her
voice floated out over the resort, where the Detroit pilgrims in search
of a miracle were staying. Crippled by polio for 14 years, she too had
traveled to the Philippines seeking a miracle, although unlike some of
the others neither her life nor her living depended on finding one. She
teaches voice at the Clarkston Conservatory of Music and sings pro-
fessionally, mostly in churches.

"For myself, if I never get out of this wheelchair, I have a full life.
I have my family, and I have my singing. I have never felt that I am a
cripple." Still, she said wistfully, "It would be nice to be able to wash
my own windows."

Connie Brubaugh was only one of 111 persons from the Detroit area
who left on Monday, October 2, 1967, on a chartered Caledonia Air-
ways plane from Windsor, Ontario, Canada, for the 36-hour flight to
Manila. These pilgrims, ranging from seven to 68 years old and for the
most part declared incurable by their doctors, made the trip in two
stages, with a 24-hour stopover in Honolulu. They were accompanied
on the 11,000-mile trip by two nurses and one unnamed doctor. The
cost of the round trip was $658 per person, much less than the $1,400
standard fare. It included 10 days in the Philippines.

The *Detroit Free Press* sent along a reporter, Gary Blonston, who
was not permitted to travel with or at first even to talk with the men,
women, and children who sought healings from Tony Agpaoa and
other Filipino spirit healers. Because he is a good reporter, he eventually talked with them anyway. Harold Sherman, who financed some of
the photographic supplies and who thought he had made arrangements
with Joe Ruffner to join the group in Manila, also was kept on the outside.

Even before the journey started, it had begun to read like an old-fashioned cloak-and-dagger melodrama, with the pilgrims frequently appearing to play the role of willing victims.

The flight was arranged by Joseph Ruffner, a 47-year-old former steel plant inspector from Wyandotte, Michigan, who was healed by Antonio Agpaoa in November, 1966, after spending 11 years [sic] in a wheelchair. Ruffner had been injured in an industrial accident, which left him crippled and in great pain. [It was footnoted that Harold Sherman had written about Ruffner in *Fate,* August, 1967.]

The pilgrims' faith in the healer had been greatly enhanced by a face-to-face meeting with "Dr. Tony" in the Detroit area several days before their departure for the Philippine Islands. Tony had made a special trip to Detroit to explain that he could not demonstrate his powers in America because he was being watched by the "authorities." He did pray silently with the pilgrims, his eyes shut, arms outspread, palms up; and he did shake their hands. He cut several thicknesses of adhesive tape with his hand and with his tongue and somehow confirmed the faith of all these believers, some of whom were being discouraged by their doctors and their families from making the trip.

One woman said, "I felt as though I should see a halo around him or something. He was just an ordinary man, but the crippled people—the ones who went on the flight—they looked to him with such hope. Grown men had tears in their eyes."

And they managed to believe with Mrs. Ruffner, who said, "I don't think God would let all these people down."

It is easy to understand why the pilgrims traveled the 11,000 miles to the Philippines despite the expense and the physical hardship and even when their friends and relatives called them fools. They believed the 28-year-old Agpaoa could heal cancers and deformities that organized medicine in the United States says are incurable, and because they believed, they went. They all said they had been told by doctors there was no hope for them, that as long as they lived, their hands would be useless knots or their knees never would bend again or they would die. As one passenger said when they embarked, "When a doctor has said there is no more hope and you hear of someone who offers one last chance the money is not important."

Dr. Tony represents a search as old as history, the search for relief from illness and suffering through some agency beyond the power of man.

The pilgrims also had been encouraged by stories of previous "cures." Gary Blonston of the *Detroit Free Press* and Al Stark of the *Detroit News* both reported the story told by P.L. Katigbak, the Philippines' general manager of the Detroit-based Parke-Davis Co. This 56-year-old medical doctor says, "Actually, I am a little ashamed to tell this story but considering what actually happened . . . in a split second my tooth was out with no pain. Unbelievable."

Katigbak practiced medicine for 10 years before joining Parke-Davis. He is the cousin of a Philippine national senator and was in medical class at Manila's University of Santo Tomas with three men who have since served as Philippine secretaries of health. He is one of the few medical men in the islands who expresses any faith in the bare-handed "psychic surgery."

In January, 1967, he was visiting his hometown, Batangas, when a broken tooth began to bother him. His family suggested that a healer remove it. To please them he agreed.

"It was amazing," Katigbak says.

The healer put salt into a glass of water, covered it with a handkerchief, prayed over it, and then had him gargle with the solution.

"Then he reached in—I could feel his fingernails—and it was out. There was no pain at all."

Katigbak said the healer who works only on teeth "appeared to suffer pain himself after the operation, but I felt nothing."

The Filipino Spiritist healers and Antonio Agpaoa in particular gained world-wide publicity in 1967 after a number of patients declared they had performed internal operations, making deep incisions with their bare hands, without the use of instruments and "through the power of God" to heal them.

The Spiritists, organized into the Union Spiritista Cristiana de Filipinas, have 500 chapel-like healing centers in the islands. There are 24 "spiritual surgeons" who are recognized by the group, and stories of miracle cures are common in the Philippines, where faith healing by Spiritists flourishes.

However, Tony is a renegade from the Spiritist cult. Although they grudgingly admit he has the "power" to heal, they have disowned him because they say he has been corrupted. They charge that he has accepted large gifts of money and trips to the United States from his patients and that he neglects the religious rites that the Spiritists practice. These rites consist of colorful religious rituals of singing and praying and reciting the scriptures as the operations are in progress. "Dr. Tony" does not do this.

Filipino doctors disagree with the judgment of the Spiritists. One eye specialist who watched Tony perform an operation for cataracts branded him "a complete fake." His detractors charge that his operations are a "parlor magician's trick effected with chicken entrails and expert palming."

There are many others who say Dr. Tony's so-called psychic surgery is easily explained. They say he uses sleight-of-hand and the power of suggestion, that all the preparations, the meditations are calculated to build suspense and to have an hypnotic effect upon the patient and the audience.

After stepping up to the outstretched patient Tony makes an "instinctive diagnosis." If the disease is obvious he goes right to work. Sometimes his diagnosis reveals troubles the patient never knew he had.

Tony's closed hands hover momentarily over the patient's skin; then they begin to knead. Photographs of the surgery show Tony's fingers buried deep in abdominal flesh. Some on-the-spot witnesses and some students of the many motion and still pictures taken of these operations claim that Tony holds a small bag of animal blood or blood-colored fluid in his hand and that during the kneading of the flesh, this fluid is squeezed out to flood the skin. Another suggestion is that Tony uses phenophthalein dissolved in water to make a clear solution. Baking soda, also, is clear when dissolved in water. But mixed together they make a red liquid. The skeptics believe that the "alcohol" used so freely in psychic surgery may be one mixture and the cotton swab may contain the other.

These skeptics then suggest that the palmed bag which no longer contains any fluid and which actually is a thin membrane, like a pig bladder, is unrolled and flattened out across the patient's skin. This slimy blood-colored tissue makes it appear that the internal organs are exposed.

Moments later this membrane is again gathered up into a ball in Tony's hand and becomes the tumor just removed from the interstices. At this time Tony's hands stop pressing into the patient's abdomen, and the "incision" disappears. The "blood" is wiped away, and, of course, there is no scar.

They say it could be done this way.

It also is suggested that in some cases Tony actually uses a concealed razor blade and in these cases the incision does not close immediately and the patients have reported feeling pain. There are scars at

such times, but Tony explains them by saying he has to leave the incision open to allow drainage.

And so the believers believe, and the doubters explain, complain,
and threaten legal action.

The Detroit pilgrims landed in Manila on October 5 and were immediately driven away in 25 taxis—at a reported fare of $50 per cab.
It was first stated by a Philippine news service dispatch that they were
headed for Baguio City, but newsmen seeking to check on the group
found they were not there, and Agpaoa's residence, which is new, impressive and built on two levels into the side of the mountain, was
deserted.

While local newsmen sought to trace the vanished visitors the *Manila
Daily Mirror* took a dim view of the whole proceedings: "They [the
pilgrims] deserve nothing but sympathy from us, but the purported
faith healer is something else again. It is a wonder that authorities have
allowed him to practice his dubious science, one result of which has
been to create an image of the Philippines abroad as a center of medical
quackery. It is up to the medical associations, if they will, to put an end
to this shameful business by prodding the authorities to action." The
paper also took this occasion to point out that Tony Agpaoa was con-
victed of illegal medical practices and fined $250 or $1,000 (according
to which account you read) in 1959 and would be prosecuted again if
he treated the visitors.

And so the chase was on!

The pilgrims switched routes outside Manila Friday to keep a secret
rendezvous with the young healer at Cresta Ola, a seaside resort in La
Union province between Baguio City and the South China Sea. Police
said Agpaoa had been missing from his Baguio home since Thursday,
the day the group arrived in Manila.

They were, of course, soon located, and a member of the Philippine
Police Constabulary, the national police, took up his post outside the
hotel, padding around in sneakers and a camouflage uniform with a
stubby sub-machine gun tucked under his arm. He and several other
policemen were there—officially to protect the American visitors from
such menaces as thieves—but some of the pilgrims apparently believe
they were there to arrest the healers. One Detroiter said, "If Tony
Agpaoa walked in here, they might just cut him down. Life is very
cheap down here, and the government doesn't like Tony."

On the other side of the coin it was reported that observers from the
Philippine Medical Association and the government's board of medical

examiners were barred from watching Dr. Tony's ministrations by husky guards, who forced them away from the hotel.

Dr. Joe G. Molano, chairman of the board of medical examiners, returned to Manila to seek police aid in investigating Agpaoa's work. Molano, Dr. Alejandro Gaerlan, a medical board member, and Dionisio Milanes, the board's legal counsel, were turned away from Cresta Ola by Ruffner.

But all this did not matter to the pilgrims as they waited for their miracles. Not did it matter that "Dr. Tony" has only a fourth-grade education and that he is accused of being a fake and a quack.

Whether for fear of the constabulary or of the mud roads, which are dangerous in the rain and bumpy full of chuck holes, wet or dry, or for other reasons, few of the pilgrims strayed far from the hotel. They did use the lovely beach, and they did use the swimming pool.

And for whatever reason, the healers stole in and out of the hotel secretly, usually at night, to perform their surgery.

From five to seven persons were crowded into 18- by 12-foot rooms, and almost all treatments took place at night without warning. If a patient was asleep, the healers just passed on to the next room. As a consequence the pilgrims, anxious not to miss the healing treatments they had traveled 11,000 miles to obtain, tried to stay awake all night, and as the days passed, weariness, tension and discouragement set in.

The Cresta Ola isn't a bad hotel for a country where a maid earns only $3.50 a month. But to Americans seven beds, six inches apart, in one room and 110 to 115-degree daytime temperature add up to discomfort.

A 20-watt light bulb dangling from the ceiling in each hotel room did little to cheer their nighttime vigils. After it was all over and the pilgrims had begun to talk, they mentioned another of the hotel's disadvantages—its odor.

"It was just plain putrid," Mrs. Townsend said.

"My pillow smelled like there was a dead chicken inside," Mr. Babiuk said.

However, none of these reports of discomfort and anxiety, of poor care and inadequate facilities leaked out of the pilgrims' hideout. Late in September as takeoff day approached Joe Ruffner had been under increasing pressure from newspaper, radio and TV reporters. In response to their insistent questions concerning names, addresses and medical histories of patients making the trip he had become defensive and ruled that no one would be permitted to contact the patients. He also ordered the patients to talk to no one. And it appears from some of the reports that as disappointment and dissatisfaction grew, he even ordered the patients not to talk to each other!

Meanwhile the reports coming back to the United States toward the end of the first week in October concerning the Detroit pilgrimage were cheerful and optimistic. After their initial silence, the travelers began to speak guardedly to newsmen.

Joey Sutika's mother reported that her crippled son needed ordinary shoes for the first time in his life as a result of treatment he had received. Joey, who has been a victim of spina bifida since birth, was the 1964 Torch Drive poster boy. Charlotte Sutika reported that her son now could stand normally and that he had taken three steps. She said she would not allow him to take more because he had no walking shoes. Nor would she allow the boy to be seen or say which of the faith healers was responsible for his improvement.

She appeared convinced that Joey had undergone a profound physical change. "I didn't believe until after I got here but I did believe after the first treatment Joey had. I would sell everything I own to do it again. This was our last hope," she said.

A *Detroit News* headline for October 9 read: "New Psychic Cures Claimed in Philippines."

Dan Pas, 20, of Wyandotte, and David Williams, 32-year-old Negro from Detroit, both declared themselves much helped. Pas said he has had speech and memory limitations since he was struck in the face with a baseball bat when he was seven years old. But on October 8 he told a reporter in clear and steady language that he now spoke much better and that the change was Tony's work.

"I couldn't see what he was doing," Dan said, "but my father told me he operated here and here." He pointed to his temples. He also said the healer operated without pain or anesthesia on his neck to free him of stuttering.

Williams, a cripple who is only four feet six inches tall, said he began to walk again after being treated by Agpaoa. He dramatically threw away his crutches before Philippine TV news cameras, a newspaper reported. Williams said he had lost the ability to walk 18 months previously after an operation. His problems apparently stem from childhood rickets.

Williams said he felt like a new man. "I don't know exactly what happened. I was in deep prayer. But it's something greater than men can understand. I am an electrical engineer, and I used to have to see to believe. Educated people cannot understand this kind of thing."

Billy Kernosek, a 14-year-old Dearborn boy suffering from muscular dystrophy, reportedly had begun to walk unaided for the first time in two years after treatment by Agpaoa. However, Gary Blonston wrote from the scene that Billy "is unsteady and still obviously handicapped." Back home Billy Kernosek's doctor, Dr. A. Jackson Day, said that if the boy had improved it probably was a "temporary remission brought on psychosomatically"; and Billy's mother said she doubted that Billy had been cured by the faith healer. She said Billy walked in the yard every day last summer, but "lately his condition has worsened and he hasn't been able to walk."

Billy Kernosek was accompanied on the trip by his uncle, the Rev. Fr. Kernosek, a Roman Catholic priest from Romulus, Michigan. According to him, Agpaoa made an incision in Billy's body, and the next morning Billy walked upstairs alone to the resort's dining room for breakfast.

A 38-year-old Detroit woman who wished her name withheld started the trip on crutches after U.S. doctors told her the only way they could end her constant pain was with a bone fusion which would put her into a wheelchair for the rest of her life. When Gary Blonston saw her at Cresta Ola she could bend her knees for the first time in years and was walking hesitantly.

Blonston wrote: "It was the first time Dr. Tony had allowed himself to be seen by anyone outside the nervous circle of patients and protectors, who for the past week have helped him work undercover after dark in the hotel by the sea. But I arrived seconds too late to see his treatment."

His patient sat on the edge of a steel cot. The sheets were stained with something mud-colored and a basin of water stood nearby . . . the faith healer moved forward to help the patient up. The woman gained her feet, and Dr. Tony told her, "Go ahead. Walk."

She took a few steps and laughed: "I can bend my knees. I haven't been able to for years."

After a week of hide-and-seek Blonston finally managed to witness a treatment. "Dr. Tony" had promised to perform an operation while Blonston watched. But before he could do this, Tony said he must visit Wilbur Shadley, a 57-year-old man from Manchester, Michigan, who reportedly had cancer of the lung and several other afflictions.

Tony knelt near Shadley's head and put his hand on him, then waved and shook his fingers over various parts of Shadley's body. Having moved to the foot of the bed he placed his thumb between Shadley's second and third toes. Suddenly Shadley arched up from the bed, moaning in apparent pain. Then he relaxed once more. Tony said his action (producing a kind of electric current) "puts the body in balance."

"We are balancing his body. He is in imbalance because of disease. We must balance the Yin and the Yang. It will shake all his muscles and stimulate his circulation."

It appeared to Blonston that Tony was jamming his thumb hard into the tender skin between the man's toes, which might make anyone jump. But Mr. Shadley said, "It feels warm between my toes. I feel relieved."

When it came time for Dr. Tony to keep his promise, the operation didn't come off after all—for want of some cotton.

Tony had selected a large woman who said she had calcium deposits on the bottom of her stomach. Tony laid his hands on her in a preliminary examination and his fingers were hidden in the loose flesh of her abdomen. Then having decided to operate he left the room to seek cotton and towels. Returning a few minutes later, he said they had been packed.

The Detroiters were leaving for Manila and a plane one hour later.

Tony had told the reporter he needed the cotton only to swab away blood during his treatments but now stated that without it he could not operate.

On the eve of their departure more and more of the pilgrims were willing to talk. Most of them said they had been helped.

One man said, "I don't think we have more than seven or eight people at this point who feel they have not been helped to any degree."

There have been no miracle cures, they said, no sudden changes in physical appearance, no dramatic new abilities; but there have been changes. At any rate, on the eve of their departure for home they seemed happy and confident of a better life.

Certainly they were disregarding the stories that claim Antonio Agpaoa is a master psychologist but a surgical fraud.

All things come to an end, and on Sunday, October 15, the chartered flight brought the pilgrims back to the Windsor airport. They had boarded this same plane on this same spot two weeks before—filled with faith and hope. Now it was over. Now some of them were crying, some were still on crutches and in wheelchairs, some still clung to their faith in an expected cure and some believed they had found what they sought.

One of the few who firmly believes he was cured by Tony is David Williams. He hobbled through the Canadian Customs with the stewardess carrying his crutches. Though newspaper accounts said he "threw away his crutches" a photo shows the girl carrying them as she walks beside him. (Williams' doctor reportedly stated that Williams could walk before he went to the Philippines but they had advised him to use crutches as his leg bones are not strong and are liable to break.)

[It should also be noted here that Williams later tried to sue Ruffner, a Detroit TV commentator, a TV station, and two other men for telecasting films shot of his treatment in the Philippines. He claimed they show him disrobed and display the "deformed portions" of his body. He refuses comment on his "cure" and once told friends he planned to write an "exposé" of the trip.]

Charlotte Sutika seemed distraught and had nothing to say as her son Joey was carried from the plane. It had been reported that the boy was cured, but now when a TV newsman inquired, his mother shook her head and replied tearfully, "No."

Later the *Detroit Free Press* reported that Mr. and Mrs. Sutika said they had caught Tony faking an operation on Joey.

A middle-aged woman who was suffering from arthritis and diabetes and still is suffering from arthritis and diabetes said, "I feel worse, lots worse. He pulled and twisted my knees. He may be a faith healer, but arthritis isn't his specialty."

Stanley Babiuk, who had lost more than 20 pounds through fasting in order to prepare himself spiritually for the cure, told how an assistant treated him in the wrong part of the body for an ailment he never had.

Doris Chandonnet stated she had concealed her disappointment in a useless operation given to her so that other patients would not lose faith. She described this operation saying: "Tony had one hand in me but didn't cut anything . . . he took something from the assistant and threw it down on me. I heard a wet loud splash and blood appeared. He stretched something over my stomach like a membrane and I could see blood, but no hole . . . As to what they removed, he told me it was a tumor. I call it a gizzard."

Mr. Chandonnet told how the filth, stench and inadequate care of the patients appalled him. He said he spent his time helping the neglected patients leave their beds at Cresta Ola for baths and bowel movements.

John Kushay, 50, who had been crippled from ruptured discs and an unsuccessful bone fusion operation on his back, was one of the happy ones. He said, "This is the first time I've walked without pain in seven years."

A man who had accompanied his wife suffering from polyneuritis in her hands and feet said he is reserving judgment. "I personally think she's better, but it will take time before we really know. We went over believing in God and we came back believing in God."

Another couple disagreed as to whether they had been helped. Lisle Townsend, 59, is paralyzed from the waist down. When he left, he had told an interviewer he expected to walk down the ramp when he got back. Although he was still in his wheelchair, his faith was unshaken, and he said, "I'll be up in about three months."

His wife, Jane, who underwent an operation for a bad kidney said, "One moment I'm a complete skeptic, the next moment I'm just the opposite. We'll have to wait and see what the doctors say now. I will wait to see lab tests to prove to me there was a healing."

She termed the trip "quite an experience" but advised others who are considering the trip to wait until medical records have been fully checked on the group.

When interviewed a week later by the *Free Press* Jane Townsend reportedly said she had been warned while in the Philippines that she would "be excluded from the group" if she persisted in her efforts to get the pilgrims together to discuss the disappointments and the lies.

Most of the passengers disembarking from the plane were tense and tight-lipped. And so were the 250 persons who waited for them. The usual answer to reporters' questions was, "No comment."

Billy Kernosek tried to convince no one. Despite claims that he was one of those cured Billy was still wearing his aluminum braces as he lurched away from the plane. He was matter-of-fact when he said, "I feel fine. The trip was a little bit like a vacation."

George Allen, 22, partially paralyzed from the waist down as the result of an automobile accident said, "I'm $1,000 poorer and $1,000 smarter. But I don't want to see anyone go through what I went through."

He described a series of eight operations by Agpaoa and his disciples, which he said left his condition unchanged. "Each time an incision was made there was a strong odor like something spoiled. I don't think my blood stinks. I heard they diagnosed instinctively, but the first thing they asked me was, 'What's the matter with you?'"

Allen brought home the blood-splattered shorts he had worn during the operations and turned them over to the *Free Press,* which had the blood analyzed by an independent laboratory. The lab reported it was animal blood.

On Sunday, October 29, the *Free Press* reported the death of Wilbur Shadley, the Manchester contractor afflicted with lung cancer who had had his Yin and Yang balanced by Tony earlier in the month.

Mrs. Shadley said, "I don't feel any bitterness, not one bit. This is a free country, and we made the decision to go and that was it. I don't think Tony is worse than the doctors we've got right here. At least he makes your mind feel good."

As James Osberg, for 10 years science and aviation writer for the *Chicago American* and now free-lancing, who accompanied the group and part of the time acted as spokesman said, "These were people who had been told their cases were terminal. They turned to faith healing for a possible solution."

That concluded Ms. Fuller's article. She tagged an editor's note on the end, which stated: "Our long years of reading on this subject indicate that some small percentage of those hopelessly ill who turn to faith healing do receive cures. It would seem the problem facing the scientific and medical world today is why those few receive miraculous cures and why the thousands of others making the same search do not receive a miracle. What makes the difference? In all our reading we find no answer to this question. Nor do we find that anyone at all is seeking an answer."

Those of us on the outside peering through the looking glass of Fuller's article can see there's a great deal to this entire phenomenon. Her article merely scratches the surface of the effects on one group of people. There's more to that trip—such as the confrontation between the believers and the detractors and the incredible working conditions imposed upon the healers as well as the patients.

Quijano De Manila, a reporter for the *Philippines Free Press,* wrote of the "antique war between faith and science" in an article printed October 21, 1967.

Noting that the "positions of the antagonists were somewhat reversed," De Manila explained that the scions of science balked at the scientific method and concealed the truth under a guise of obscure legality while the "forces of superstition" demanded the "audacities of experimentation."

Journalist James Osberg and Ruffner took it on themselves to represent the psychic surgeon to the Medical Board of Examiners. They did so to "get the PMA off our backs."

De Manila's account of the actual confrontation between the professionals and the healer's representatives has been verified by a number of persons present at the time, including one hostile witness. Here is his story:

The PMA was notified, and the Philippine Board of Medical Examiners—Drs. José Molano, Arturo Tolentino, Jr., and Julia Presbitero —arrived on Monday morning in response to the challenge to witness an operation in which a patient's body would be opened without the use of surgical instruments, diseased material removed from inside it, and the wound closed without leaving a scar. James Osberg of the pilgrim group offered himself as guinea pig for the demonstration and promised that the performing "practitioner" would wear a short-sleeved shirt, could be watched at close range, could be photographed or filmed by the watchers who would include, besides the medical examiners, a group of La Union doctors and the press.

Osberg's one condition was that no legal action was to be taken against the practitioner on the basis of that demonstration and that the American pilgrim group was to be spared further harassment. Osberg knew that, since opening a human body constituted medical practice, the practitioner could be liable to prosecution: "We came in good faith and we have been served in good faith, and we cannot allow a situation to arise that will expose the practitioner to retaliation by the government or the medical authorities after we are gone. That would be a breach of confidence on our part. We cannot have him subject to legal liability that we are responsible for in the first place."

He was offering himself as guinea pig because he had complete medical records with the Veteran's Administration, against which the results of the demonstration could be checked. His ailment was cystic fibrosis of the bladder; he had been treated by Agpaoa several months before and had experienced relief; he no longer had to get up four or five times

a night to urinate. The demonstration would thus be a further treatment.

If he was bluffing, it would have been easy enough to call his bluff,
but the strange thing is that it was the medical examiners who inter-
posed one objection after another until their conference with Osberg
bogged down in wordily professed concern over legalities.

The medical examiners' objection was originally that they didn't
want "our hands tied." If they consented to watch the demonstration
and saw anything illegal, they would have to demand prosecution. Apparently a bit hard of understanding they had to have it explained to
them over and over that Osberg was not asking for "perpetual immunity" for the practitioner, as they kept insisting, but only immunity from
legal action for that particular demonstration. When this finally registered, they developed other qualms. They may be forgiven the fear
of risking their dignity—this was an "international" case; the eyes of
the world were upon them—but not their fear of any normal, let alone
scientific, curiosity. All this was to them just witchcraft and superstition
and racketeering.

Osberg then explained that Agpaoa had been under observation for
two weeks at Tokyo University, by Dr. Hiroshi Motoyama, a Ph.D.
and director of the Institute of Religious Psychology. Dr. Motoyama
had apparently not considered it beneath his dignity to study the
Filipino faith healer, and he had written a report of his observations
and submitted it for analysis to Duke University, where he used to
teach.

Osberg promised to make the Motoyama study on Agpaoa available
to the Philippine Board of Medical Examiners, plus the medical histories of all the patients in the American pilgrim group who claimed
to have been cured, plus the subsequent reports of their respective
physicians after they returned home, plus all the high speed 16mm
color films he had taken of operations.

"I want," said Osberg, "to make available to you the widest avenue
of research, so that there may be a meaningful investigation of faith
healing." [Osberg's sincere and noble attempt at scientific study was
not authorized by Agpaoa; had Osberg been taken up on the challenge,
a strong chance existed the healer would have embarrassed him.]

If there was an objection to Osberg as the guinea pig in the demonstration, he was open to some other proposal. A member of the doctors'
group then proposed that either of two patients he had—one with
shrapnel in his body, the other with a stone in his kidney, and both

with x ray records—might make a more acceptable patient for the dem- onstration. Would Osberg agree to the doctors' providing the patient?

Amazingly, Osberg not only agreed but he modified his immunity condition. The practitioner would open the patient's body without use of surgical instruments, remove either shrapnel or the stone, turn over the object to the doctors for examination, close the wound without a scar, and then submit the patient for x raying to prove that the shrapnel or the stone had really been removed. If the practitioner should use any surgical instrument, or if the matter removed proved to be other than the shrapnel or stone, or if the wound left a scar, then he would be subject to arrest right on the spot.

That's incredible enough; what's even more incredible is that the medical examiners backed out from such a proposal. If they really wanted to prosecute the faith healers, here was their chance. But their original objection widened. At first they were objecting to not prosecut- ing on the basis of the demonstration; they were now objecting to the demonstration itself. The demonstration would in itself be illegal, and they could not be a party or witness to it—a position they surely didn't come all the way from Manila to state. The suspicion thus became strong that they had come to watch but got cold feet. Were they afraid they might not be able to explain what they saw?

Joseph Ruffner, the real leader of the group, kept telling Osberg: "Come on, they're not serious. We're just wasting our time." But Osberg stayed and tried to save the demonstration. It was the medical authorities who scrupled, split hairs, and finally walked out.

Those who feel that the Philippines are primitive and un- sophisticated should note that their orthodox medical groups are every bit as sophisticated in their dogma as are those in the United States. On the other hand, the facts are not clear about Tony Agpaoa and psychic surgery. There's still much more to this topic.

I spoke briefly with Blonston of the *Detroit Free Press,* and he explained that Agpaoa had some "tough body guard types" keeping tabs on the reporters during that hectic pilgrimage.

"When I was filing my last story, the one about how Tony dug his fingernails into Wilbur Shadley's toes, I was in a phone booth outside the hotel, and these three goons came up. They were menacing enough for my money, so I beat it out of there."

Blonston worked on the story of that pilgrimage to the point of being sick of it. I asked him how many of the pilgrims actually remained satisfied that they were helped.

"About half of them. The other half has some doubts, and I'd say about a third of that latter half are very unhappy."

The inconsistencies in this entire matter are enough to drive a researcher into another field. What about fraud? Charges of fraud go back much further than the 1967 pilgrimage. Every phenomenal thing in history has a share of bogus allegations.

The public outcry regarding Agpaoa's faking and deception was made from two prime sources. First a film team claimed that they had uncovered an entire ring of fraud, and later talk show host Joe Pyne claimed that he had "proved" the whole thing was a hoax.

Getting to the essence of the first series of charges called for a meeting with Henry Belk, millionaire department store chain owner from Charlotte, North Carolina, who is a self-proclaimed psychic researcher. Belk is a proud, keenly intelligent man, whose mannerisms and speech are often abrupt and abrasive. He has been accused of clouding his research with his own ego, which may be the case with all researchers. Belk has been digging for truth in phenomena since his school days at Duke University in the late 1930s. He *knows* that the phenomenon of healing is genuine, having experienced and witnessed it many times. He is well aware of the fact that on certain occasions Tony Agpaoa has performed genuine psychic surgery because he personally observed and tested the operations.

"Why, I held a boy's intestines in my own hands. Tony didn't cut anything, he just parted the skin and the intestine just came out of the boy's body. When he was done—he cut off a section several inches long and somehow fused it back together—it went back in with one big slush."

However, despite his subjective knowledge, Belk is deeply chagrined at his role in opening the doors to the Filipino healers.

"I have caused a lot of innocent people, desperate people, to be fleeced," he said with obvious regret. He feels he helped Agpaoa to "bilk Americans out of more than $300,-000 over the past several years." It was Belk who financed much of the early research on Tony, including the visit by Dr. Motoyama and Tony's visit to Japan. He also contributed a sizable sum to Tony's church in 1966.

"He's a double agent," Belk exclaims about Agpaoa. "When his spirit goes on vacation, he can't do anything, so he's dishonest about it and perpetrates a hoax much of the time."

Belk believes also that much of the controversy is due to the kinds of people who visit the Philippines. He contends there are four motivations for visitors:

"First, there are the religious fanatics and all-out believers, who will believe anything and everything; second, there are those people looking for a cheap operation that won't leave a scar; third, there are those who want to buy a healer and horde him for themselves for research purposes or otherwise; and finally, there's a handful of serious, objective students."

I would add still another category of visitors, a group that is perhaps second most numerous to the desperately ill—the phenomena seekers. These are persons who travel far and wide to witness seances, life-readings, voodoo rites, psychic surgery, mediumship, and other phenomena and delude themselves into thinking that they are obtaining the secrets of the universe.

Among the several investments Belk made in the course of his research in the Philippines was the hiring of a professional camera team, Elgin Ciampi and his wife, Renée duBonnet Ciampi, a psychic, to film the various operations. The Ciampis claimed that they uncovered a vast ring of healing fraud, that all psychic surgery is faked, that they had proof on film and were barely able to escape the Philippines with their lives, when it was learned they had discovered the con-game.

After a lengthy court battle Belk finally obtained copies of the films that he had financed, and he set out to show them to anyone who cared to hear his arguments that Tony Agpaoa

was a double dealer. I saw the Ciampi "proof" when Belk
showed his film at a 1972 Spiritual Frontiers Fellowship convention in Chicago. The audience reaction to the films and
Belk's allegations was noteworthy.

In the picture Renée Ciampi goes to a Filipino meat market,
which the Ciampis claimed supplied the healers with necessities
for faking, and bought a piece of membrane, probably pig bladder. She then gave an obviously amateurish demonstration of
a faked psychic surgery. When several of the people present
protested to Belk that her fakery and Tony's operations weren't
at all alike, Belk replied:

"Why, Tony's had lots more practice, that's all."

The slowest of slow motion did not show conclusively that
Agpaoa's various operations were faked. Several people protested that Belk was proving psychic surgery rather than expos-
ing fraud.

A man asked: "Why belabor the point? Why dwell on fakery, if indeed there has been fakery. One white crow is all that's
needed to prove they're not all black—and you've admitted
having encountered that white crow, Mr. Belk."

Greta Deal, who claims a miraculous healing from Tony,
asked Belk why he thought it so important to "know how God
worked."

Belk, whose prime motive in his exposé and his research is
to get people to be more objective, answered: "We're all children of God, and He gave us minds. We should use them."

Although the Ciampi allegations were objectively aired by
Harold Sherman in *Wonder Healers of the Philippines,* Joe
Pyne's televised "investigation" of the phenomenon had a far
greater impact on public opinion.

Pyne's talk show, featuring caustic attacks on many people
and their ideas, was a highly rated program in Los Angeles. A
surprising number of people base their opinion that all psychic
surgery is faked on Pyne's show, in which a magician pulled
a rubber chicken from "inside" an obese volunteer. Raymond
Bayless, a reputable psychic researcher associated with the
Southern California Society for Psychical Research, told me

that Agpaoa was a fraud on this basis. Bayless even had a replica of the rubber chicken in his home.

Joe Pyne's "research" amounted to three days in Baguio City, where he made many enemies of the Americans seeking cures and viewed only one abdominal operation performed by Tony.

"None of us wanted him around. He was so obnoxious and negative the whole time he was there."

Olga Farhit, forty-two, of Los Angeles, gave one of the most dramatic and well-documented testimonials to the fact of psychic surgery in existence. She was a patient at Agpaoa's home when Joe Pyne conducted his highly publicized "investigation."

"Pyne watched the one and only operation he was allowed to see for only a few minutes; then he burst out of the room hollering he saw fakery. He had a medical doctor with him, Dr. Tom Humphrey. He introduced the man as a news reporter. It was obvious that Pyne had not come to study what was happening. He had his mind made up in advance. There were other medical doctors in our group, and they returned thoroughly impressed."

Ironically, Pyne could not have singled out a better time to investigate had he truly wished to be objective. Not only was Farhit's case on the docket, but Joe Ruffner hobbled in and burst out of the operating room—actually hoisting Pyne off the ground in a dramatic demonstration of the healing, as was mentioned earlier.

"Joe Pyne shouted at me," Ms. Farhit reports. "He said, 'How dare you, a doctor's wife, come here and be a part of this?' I was furious. I told him my husband had given his blessings before he died. I told him that orthodox medicine had run into a blank wall and could do nothing."

Ms. Farhit's condition was due to a mysterious and deadly deterioration of the bone marrow in her head and shoulders. The condition was first detected in her sternum and clavicle late in 1962. Biopsy and extensive tests were made at Cedars of Lebanon and Mt. Sinai Hospitals, where she received the best of medical care.

By 1965 the excruciating pain and destruction of the marrow had moved into the back of her skull. In 1966 surgeons scraped the bones in both the back and front of her head, but they were powerless to stem the spreading, unknown disease.

"In the summer of 1966 I went to the UCLA Medical Center for five days of tests. Many specialists were consulted, and finally I was told that nothing could be done. I faced permanent paralysis, more surgery, becoming a vegetable, and death. They didn't tell me how long I would live, but they agreed among themselves that I wouldn't last long."

The doomed woman was home watching television and trying to subdue her pain with prescribed narcotics when she saw a psychic that she "intuitively" wanted to meet. The psychic was Jacqueline Eastlund, and when Olga Farhit met her, the sensitive immediately stated she "saw something disturbing" about Ms. Farhit's face.

"She said she saw a healer's name . . . Tony . . . before me. She didn't know who he was, and I thought it was some local healer. When I asked, she said that he lives in the Philippines.

"I tried contacting various people who knew of Tony, and in the meantime my husband passed away."

She joined one of Dr. Bernard Jensen's tours. Jensen, a chiropractor from the San Diego area, has been a longtime advocate of Agpaoa's ability. On November 5, 1966, Ms. Farhit arrived in Baguio. She was deathly ill, and she almost turned back. Her sister Cornelia was her companion.

When she met Tony, he looked her over and said he had to meditate on her case. The following day he visited her first thing in the morning and told her that he had been informed by "the spirit" not to touch her face but to remove the disease out through her chest. The only persons she allowed to observe the operation were her sister and Dr. Jensen.

"I felt fantastic while I was lying there; something vibrant pervaded my being. Tony removed what looked like a tremendous mass of cartilage and blood. He asked my sister if she'd like to cut the diseased matter away with scissors, but she declined. When he removed his hands and the incision closed, he meditated for several minutes as we watched in curious silence. He opened his eyes suddenly and said, 'Ma'am, you are healed.' "

Agpaoa suggested she remain close to him for several days, and she complied by assisting him for a week.

"I helped him for nearly a week, and day by day I improved. He told me that when I returned I was not to have x rays taken for at least six weeks."

She watched Joe Ruffner's dramatic healing. "We all cried like babies when he walked out of that room." She also tells of a tooth extraction by Tony: "It was a terribly bad tooth, but Tony got two toothpicks and pulled it out like it was nothing. When the blood started gushing where the tooth had been, he simply reached in with his thumb, and it coagulated—instantly."

When Olga Farhit returned to Los Angeles, she felt so healthy that she couldn't stand the suspense of waiting the full six weeks for x rays. She went to St. Vincent's Hospital for a check-up and x rays after only five weeks.

"The doctor, who had been one of my surgeons, didn't want to x ray me. He said I looked so good that I should leave well enough alone. But I insisted. X rays were taken, and I had a thorough examination; even tissue samples were tested. The next day the doctor was grinning from ear to ear. 'I don't know what to say, but there's nothing left except scar tissue. It's like something went in and cleaned you out.'

"I literally had a clean bill of health, but I couldn't tell him about the Philippines, so I just asked his opinion of what happened. He said, 'It's one of the mysteries of life—God gives and God takes away.' "

As of this writing Ms. Farhit is busy, happy, and healthy, with no sign of the deadly bone marrow disease's recurring.

Taking the diseased tissue out of her chest rather than where doctors knew it existed hints broadly that this phenomenon defies physical laws in every sense. But it is much easier to at-

62 Psychic Surgery

tribute Ms. Farhit's case to "a natural remission" and Agpaoa's performance to sleight of hand and powerful psychological suggestion. It's obvious from testimony that some operations have been as phony as others are genuine.

Keep one thing forever in view—the truth; and if you do this, though it may seem to lead you away from the opinions of men, it will assuredly conduct you to the throne of God.

Horace Mann

Tony Agpaoa speaks to an audience of tourists in the chapel in his home. In the background is a brilliant-colored mural, which was painted by a former patient.

Tony Agpaoa now 35 years old, is the world's best-known psychic surgeon.

Tony removes a neck tumor from a Puerto Rican patient. People from all over the world travel to the Philippines to seek Agpaoa's help.

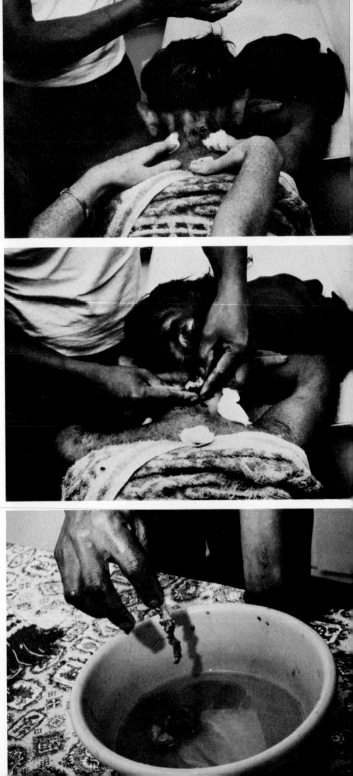

After opening the patient's neck, without the aid of instruments, Tony removes the tumor.

Tony deposits the tissue into a bowl near the operating table.

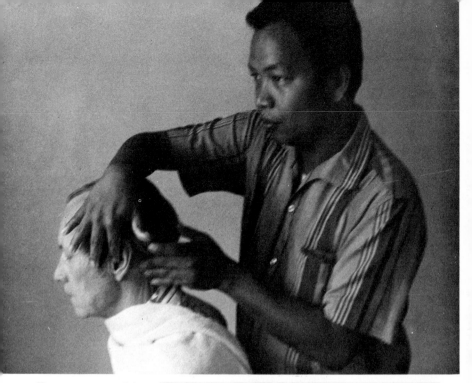

Tony massages John Hall's ear and throat. John Hall had been unable to hear, and Tony diagnosed psychically which ear was dysfunctional. Tony later removed pieces of hard, marble-like tissue, and Hall's hearing was restored.

Tony gives magnetic healing to a woman with a serious case of leg ulcers. When she left the Philippines, after six months of treatment, the ulcers had disappeared.

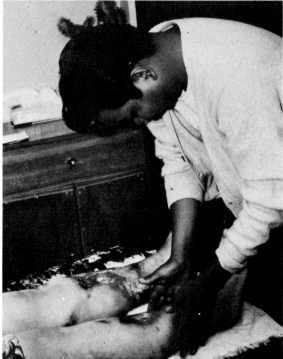

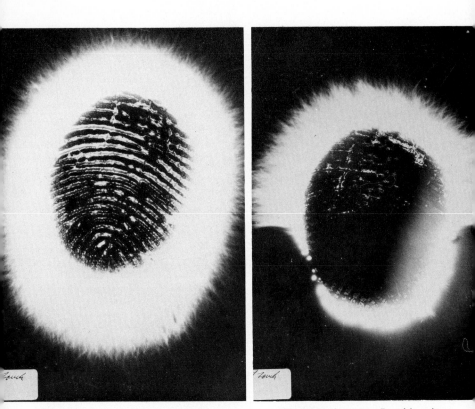

Fingertip of person A, very energetic.

Fingertip of person B, with a low energy level.

Photographs on these pages are examples of Kirlian photography from the laboratory of Dr. Thelma Moss, of UCLA. Shown are the fingertips of two people (A and B); one person is extremely energetic, and the other is lethargic. These photographs and others like them have been presented as evidence that there is indeed observable bodily energy transmitted by healers.

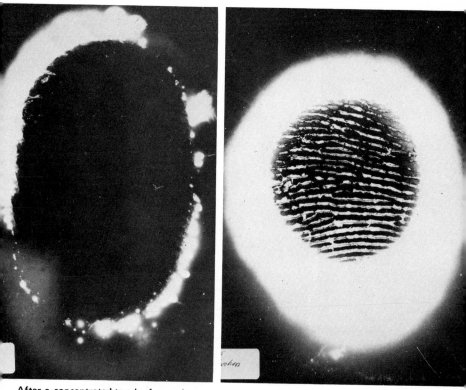

After a concentrated touch of several minutes' duration, person A's fingertip shows a depletion of energy, and . . .

. . . person B shows a dramatic increase in energy level.

Frames from Casey Kryston's motion picture of Dr. Tony's controversial operation on John Orlicki's throat. In an unbroken sequence the viewer can detect the removal of a large, tumor-like piece of tissue.

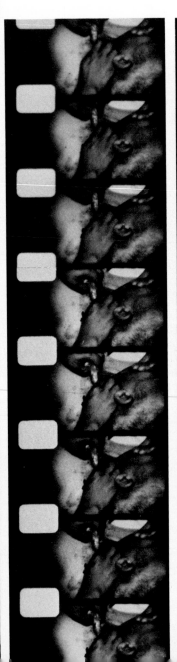
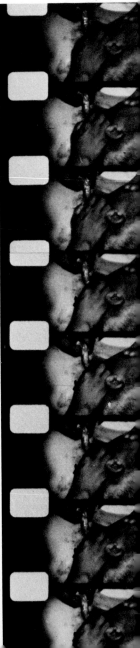

Kryston's film, which the author has seen in its entirety, is the most explicit and revealing piece of evidence of the truth of psychic surgery.

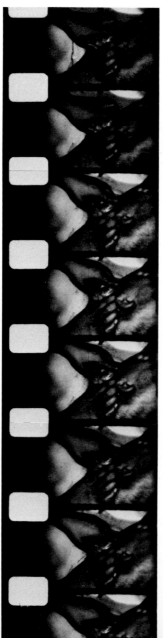

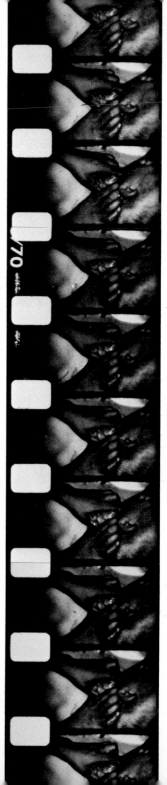

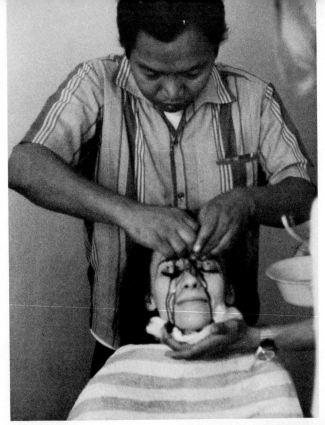

Above: Tony attempted to cure Marla Kelly's chronic headaches by means of psychic surgery, but he failed. The headaches were cured later by another psychic surgeon. Right: before operating on Mike Jablonski, a multiple sclerosis victim, Tony balanced Jablonski's yin and yang.

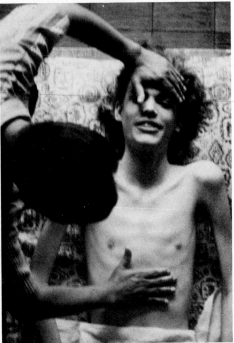

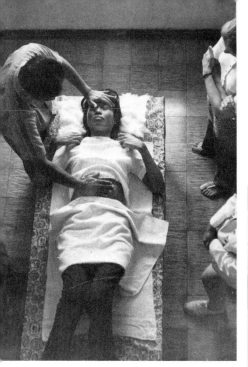

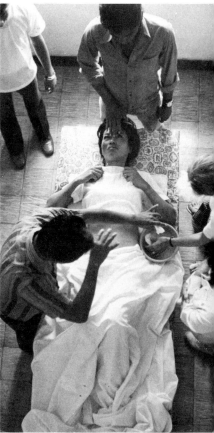

Photographs on this page show Dr. Tony's psychic operation on Dorothy Bequette. Upper left and right: the patient's yin and yang are balanced.

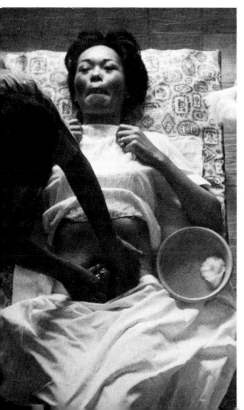

Lower left: Tony removes a massive benign tumor from her abdomen.

1

2

Kirlian photographs of three separate leaves (A, B, and C) offer evidence that human concentration affects all living things. There were obvious changes in the energy level of the leaves under controlled circumstances. 1) Leaf A freshly plucked. 2) Leaf A after being gashed with a sharp instrument. 3) Leaf A after a short period of recuperation. 4) Leaf

6

7

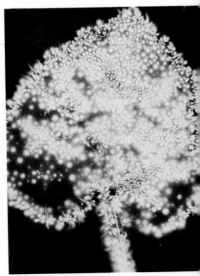

3

4

B freshly plucked. 5) Leaf B after being gashed with a sharp instrument. 6) Leaf B after being placed close to the hands of a highly energetic person (the "green thumb" effect). 7) Leaf C freshly plucked. 8) Leaf C after being gashed with a sharp instrument. 9) Leaf C after being placed close to the hands of a non-energetic person (the "brown thumb" effect).

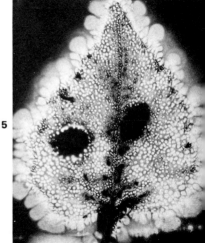

5

8

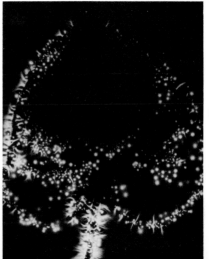

9

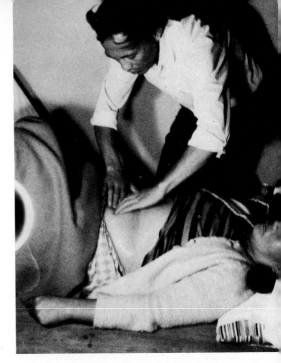

Placido, another well-known psychic surgeon, performs for the cameras. In this sequence of photos it is particularly difficult to determine whether the operation is real or fake. Its authenticity is not increased by the fact that Placido performed the same operation on the same woman for several other groups of tourists.

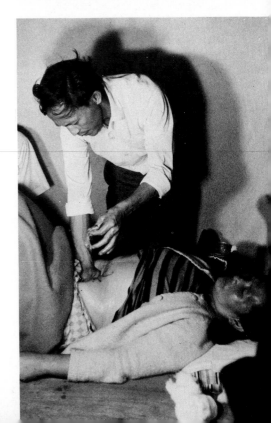

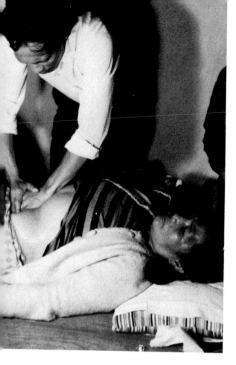
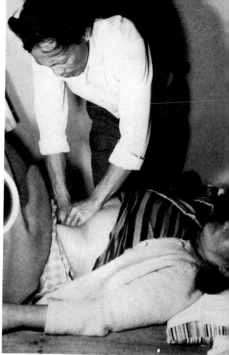
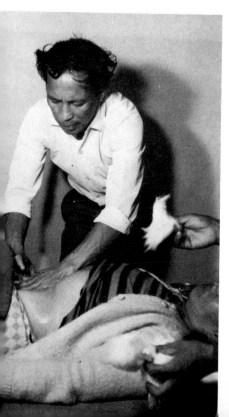
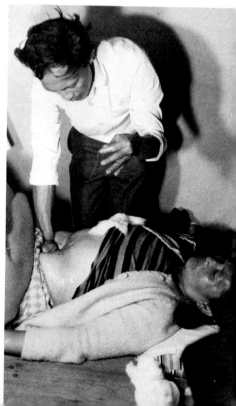

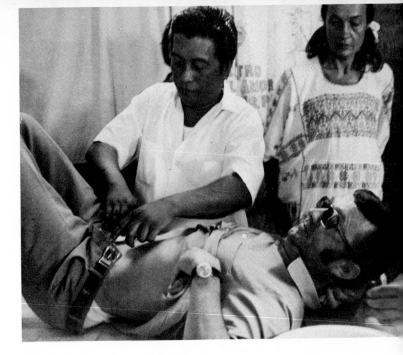

José Mercado operates psychically on Viennese psychologist Kurt Ososolbie, who remained skeptical about psychic surgery even after his operation. Mercado removed an excessive amount of pus from Ososolbie. Critics maintain that the pus was materialized, that if Ososolbie's body had actually contained that much pus, he would have been near death.

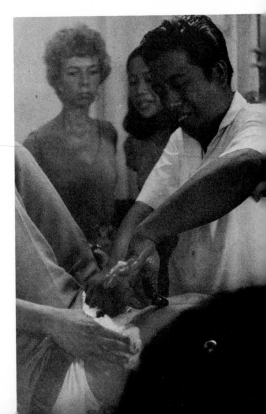

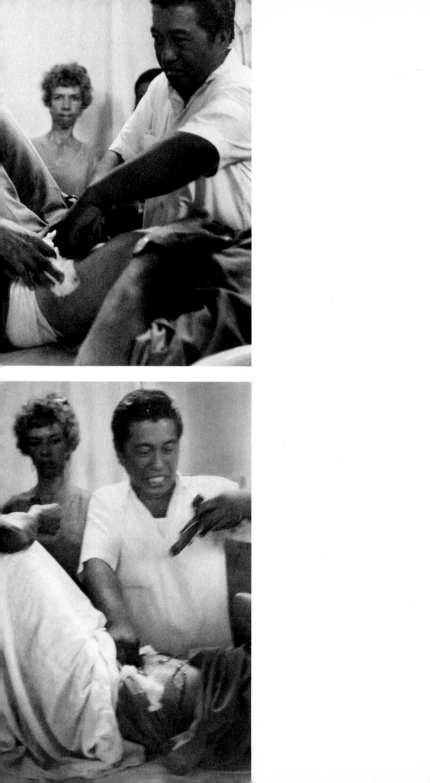

Kathryn Kuhlman, popular American faith healer, with cancer victim Julia Laurie, a recipient of one of Kuhlman's many public healings.

Kathryn Kuhlman on stage. The reports of her incredible healings draw large audiences, and her charismatic stage presence keeps them spellbound.

3 Journey to Objectivity

ONE MAY see a thousand movies and hear twice as many reports and still look forward to viewing actual psychic surgery with eager anticipation. We were eager for a firsthand view and explanation as we planned our visit to Baguio City.

The originally scheduled trip was for January, 1972. However, it was postponed until April, then until May, and finally we left on a tour in June. The postponements served us well, however. Each delay allowed us to contact new aspects of the controversy, especially those surrounding Agpaoa's practice. And each new contact with the controversy sharpened our objectivity.

One reason for our many delays was information relayed to me that Tony would refuse to cooperate with me in compiling this book. I could very well arrive in Baguio City only to be prevented from observing and interviewing.

Through Rosita Rodriguez and Agpaoa's attorney, I conveyed the message that it would be to the healer's advantage to cooperate and to let objective reporting serve his desire to be accepted as genuine. This appeal most likely would have been ineffectual had not Lucy Agpaoa journeyed to Chicago to drum up business for the Agpaoa's Diplomat Tours, a travel service. As a member of Tony's own tour I was difficult to refuse. Marlyn and I booked passage aboard the "Spiritualist Tour" to Tokyo, Manila, and Baguio City.

As the day for our departure drew close, more controversy and contradiction came to our attention.

John Orlicki, a laborer from Chicago's West Side, presented a unique case. Orlicki is Irene Przybycien's brother-in-law. Irene's case has already been viewed; she visited Tony in January, 1971, in the company of a sixteen-member group guided by her brother, Casey Kryston. Orlicki was a member of this group. Now he was making his second visit to Agpaoa's home, not for healing but to expose the healer as a fraud.

Orlicki is convinced that Agpaoa deceives, that he only

"cures" psychosomatic ailments. The rest of his family, especially Casey, Irene, and his son, Andrew Orlicki, think that it is John who has been deluded.

I was intrigued. Here was a controversy not only among people who observed the phenomenon at the same time but among members of the same family with intimate knowledge of one another's health. With comments from all the principals, I've pieced John Orlicki's story together:

"My father had cancer of the throat. He had been told by his doctor that he was terminal, and he was naturally very depressed," Andrew explained.

The tumor was large enough to be clearly visible, and John Orlicki had undergone a number of cobalt radiation treatments. In the summer of 1970 Casey Kryston saw Roy Amelio's movies of Agpaoa's operations, and he told Andrew about the phenomenon.

The two men wondered if psychic surgery could save John's life. Orlicki, a stubborn, practical man, would never have consented to visit "witch doctors," so Andy tricked him into taking a "father and son" trip to the Philippines, where John had fought during World War II.

"I didn't tell him the real reason for our trip until we were in the air, four hours on the other side of Hawaii."

The father reluctantly acquiesced to his son's wishes: "If it's a last chance, okay, I'll try anything."

Tony operated on Casey Kryston, but John Orlicki refused to watch. The healer merely placed his hands on Andrew's head and "cured" migraine headaches of long standing. Then it was John's turn.

Casey Kryston's film of Tony Agpaoa operating on John Orlicki's neck are the most vivid, obviously unfaked, pictures of psychic surgery I have ever seen. Immediately after the operation Orlicki was a changed man. His strength and energy were restored, his depression lifted. The swelling in his throat was gone. The pain was gone. His color returned with the threat of death removed.

Why does John disbelieve today?

"He believed at first," Andy explained, "but skeptics hammered at him and belittled him, so he stopped talking about it."

The doctor who diagnosed cancer had no explanation for the regression. Orlicki switched doctors, and the new physicians concluded that he did not have cancer in the summer of 1970 but that his symptoms (treated by radiation) were due to improperly fitted false teeth. John accepts this opinion, but his family does not.

Orlicki does not have the background to defend his disbelief any more than he had it to defend his faith in his personal experience. I asked him why he had not watched when Tony worked on Casey before his own operation.

"I did not want to look. Besides, I have no training to tell me what I would see. I did not like anything about the whole deal. I was afraid I would not come out alive."

Orlicki made the January, 1971, trip to "see something for myself. And I saw him [Agpaoa] fake operations." Because John Orlicki is convinced that he observed Agpaoa palm something prior to operating, Orlicki concludes that all psychic surgery, including that on his throat, is faked.

"The mind is a powerful thing, Mr. Valentine," he said, "and these people who think they are cured delude themselves into feeling better."

Orlicki is indeed untrained, but his rationalization for some of the cures attributed to the Filipino healers is identical to the explanations given by many highly qualified physicians.

"The room [in which Agpaoa operated on his throat in 1970] smelled like incense, and after an hour inside I was very relaxed. My reflexes faded, like I was on dope. Then I went back out into the fresh air, and, of course, I felt better." With these words John Orlicki rationalizes his total recovery from diagnosed throat cancer.

"He was happy in 1970, truly overjoyed, but people laughed at him, and he began to doubt," said Andrew. "I'm convinced that deep down my father does believe. It's just that he's a proud and practical man, and this thing does boggle the mind."

One month before our trip financier Morris Dreyfus visited Agpaoa and returned convinced that several of his ailments had been healed, including a diagnosed angina condition. In his excitement over the healing the seventy-six-year-old man was anxious to create a foundation to aid the healers and needy Americans who were unable to afford the trip to the Philippines.

"I also want to bring one of the healers over here to practice magnetic treatments, without opening the body and thereby not offending the AMA, which is very powerful. I am seeking the services of the best attorneys and CPAs I know to establish this foundation."

Dreyfus made this announcement informally to various small groups of friends, and his views were met with skepticism by many. The skeptics didn't phase Dreyfus: he had been to Baguio, had experienced the phenomenon. However, legal ramifications eventually caused him to abandon plans for the foundation.

When shrewd businesspeople become believers, many skeptics begin to waver. Dreyfus's testimony buoyed my confidence in this phenomenon.

While seeking support for his foundation, Dreyfus ran into a snag in the form of developer Jack Netchin. Netchin also visited the Philippines in the spring of 1972, and he testified upon his return that he had "caught Agpaoa in a red-handed fake." Netchin was bitterly disappointed in the healer. He had gone to the Philippines with hopes of verifying the phenomenon as true; his granddaughter was losing her life to an inoperable tumor in the back of her head.

Dreyfus invited Marlyn and me to a luncheon meeting to confront Netchin and banker Leonard E. Wineburgh. I was to support the veracity of psychic surgery in the face of Netchin and Wineburgh's testimony.

Jack Netchin is a dynamic, intelligent, practical man. He did not say that psychic surgery is impossible. He simply testified that he had seen Agpaoa try to fake an operation and had caught him in the act.

"Just before operating on this woman, he went into the bathroom and came out with his right hand cupped. It looked suspicious, so I grabbed his hand and turned it up—a cotton wad and bloody pieces of junk were in it."

The most interesting part of Netchin's experience was that Tony's attempt to fake an operation was so poorly executed that Netchin had no difficulty spotting it. Professional magicians have watched the healer for hours without detecting anything.

Wineburgh had just completed the sad task of burying his young wife, who died of cancer in Manila shortly after Agpaoa had performed three operations. Tony had not claimed that Mrs. Wineburgh was cured, but he had operated. This move was a definite departure from form, according to what I'd read and been told. Earlier accounts say that the healer receives a warning whenever a patient is beyond help. Harold Sherman's *Wonder Healers* tells how one elderly Filipino was brought to Agpaoa, but the healer declined to work on him, saying that the man was dying and there was nothing to be done. Mrs. Wineburgh was dying, and Tony must have known he was unable to help. At least he later confided to another American that he knew she was going to die. It is reported that he cried as he admitted, "I did all I could, but I couldn't help her."

"The operations on my wife didn't show me anything," said Wineburgh. "They looked phony to me, but I can't be absolutely sure. She wanted that last hope, and I wanted her to have it."

Netchin and Wineburgh advised Dreyfus to "wait until this thing can be scientifically verified before getting involved."

Netchin, who caught Agpaoa in poorly disguised fakery, refused to wipe such phenomena out of the realm of possibility; Netchin would be in Baguio when we arrived; he was returning to investigate further, and he invited us to join him. We decided to stay with our tour, but we promised to meet Netchin in Baguio.

The purpose of our tour, which left San Francisco June 12, 1972, was to take part in Agpaoa's Spiritualist Conference, at which the healer was hosting a regular convention. He promised to display his ability, heal members of the tour, guide them to see other healers at work, and provide speakers who would explain the phenomenon and the philosophy behind it.

Rosita Rodriguez was the tour leader and the keynote speaker for the convention.

In teeming, muggy Manila circumstances forced a change in tour plans. Half the group had to stay in the major city for an extra day, while the other half flew to Baguio. The extra day allowed us to visit the libraries of various newspapers and also the University of Santo Tomas Medical School, where Dr. Manuel Navarro is the professor of biology and medicine.

I am acquainted with Dr. Navarro through research concerning a drug called Laetrile, a synthetic amygdalin which, according to believers, works effectively in controlling cancer but which is outlawed in the United States. A full professor at a highly respected medical school, Dr. Navarro refused to join his fellows in a blanket denunciation of psychic surgery. He said that he was familiar with the claims of the healers and that he had heard several accounts of miracle healings, but he had never witnessed any surgery. "The more one learns, the more one realizes there are many unusual and unexplained realities," he said.

While in the morgue of the *Manila Times* I read some pertinent clippings. One of the first to catch my eye was a United Press International story printed November 16, 1966. It included the testimony of Joe Pyne. In light of Olga Farhit's testimony regarding the late radio and television personality, the news clipping has added interest:

> Joe Pyne, controversial Los Angeles radio personality who went to the Philippines to study the claims of faith healer Tony Agpaoa, took a dim view of Agpaoa's operations.
>
> Pyne, accompanied by Dr. Tom Humphrey, a general surgeon, spent

five days in the Philippines talking to Agpaoa, interviewing his patients, persons familiar with his activities and other faith healers in the area.

Agpaoa, or Dr. Tony, as he is called, claims to operate without using surgical instruments or anesthetic and his patients allegedly left the operating table with no ill effects or even an incision scar.

After studying Dr. Tony, Pyne concluded: "The things I saw and heard led me to believe Tony is a great showman but that he in no way has essential healing powers."

Pyne noted that tissue allegedly removed by Agpaoa from a woman was analyzed by a pathologist at a hospital and found to be hog tissue.

Pyne described an operation which he watched Agpaoa perform on a rather heavy woman who said tests had shown she had cancer.

He said that after the purported incision by Agpaoa, blood flowed, and the faith healer appeared to be kneading the flesh.

Doctor Humphrey, whose identity as a surgeon was not disclosed, was invited to reach in and feel inside the body opening.

He said afterward: "I didn't put my hand into anything. There was no incision. Now I know how he can operate and leave no incision scar."

Pyne and Humphrey concluded that Agpaoa, who kept working a blanket about as he purportedly operated, had concealed a sponge full of blood, and the blood ran into the indentations made by the kneading; then by sleight of hand he palmed off animal organs as tissue removed from the body.

Pyne said, "The tissue indeed was fresh, but it did not resemble any human tissue I've ever seen. I believe it came from a dead animal."

Pyne requested the tissue so that he might have it analyzed, but Agpaoa refused, saying he would not give it to him until after January, when his biography was released.

Pyne noted that when Agpaoa's own son became ill, he took him to a conventional hospital.

In an interview the 27-year-old faith healer claimed to have performed more than 30,000 operations with a 95 per cent rate of cure. He said that since he was seven years old, he had the feeling that God had blessed his hands.

Another faith healer told Pyne that Tony's patients often came to him after they had visited Agpaoa because he had failed to help them.

Pyne traveled to the Philippines with a group of Americans brought to Tony by Dr. Bernard Jensen, an Escondido, California, chiropractor.

Pyne described Tony as "a small, typical Filipino man with very small hands. When we shook hands, they were very soft hands. No one can accuse him of having dishpan hands. The man seems to be completely in Jensen's power."

Pyne said that Tony collected donations of $100 or more for each of his operations.

It's easy to see how a story like that influenced a tremendous number of people to regard psychic surgery as pure hokum. Few people question what they read in newspapers. Therefore, badly written stories with unsubstantiated statements often go unchallenged. The story said that tissue allegedly removed by Tony was analyzed at a hospital and found to be hog tissue. Then Pyne relates that Tony refused to give him tissue to be analyzed.

However, the article does substantiate Olga Farhit's testimony that Pyne viewed only one operation.

As a general surgeon Dr. Humphrey certainly had to disbelieve; therefore, he *expected* his touch into the wound to reveal nothing. Medical practitioners are not immune to prejudicial delusions, especially when their specified intention is to prove a phenomenon unreal. In fact, other qualified medical doctors have inserted fingers into incisions made by psychic surgeons and have verified the opening.

Unlike Jack Netchin, Pyne did not notice any sleight-of-hand attempts; still he concluded that what he saw was trickery. The news service account of his explanation of the fakery may be responsible for making Pyne's arguments appear so unfounded. Surely if a "sponge full of blood" were used, it could have been easily detected. Finally, it is absurd to assume that a television personality can tell the difference between animal and human tissue simply by looking. Such a differentiation requires microscopic chromosome structure comparisons.

Medical examiners have viewed psychic surgery. A story dated February 22, 1958, told of two MDs, members of the PMA's antiquackery committee, investigating healers:

"One healer removed a benign tumor from the nape of a patient's neck with the aid of a razor blade, bare fingers, and alcohol." Another paragraph read: "Another medium drew out a long strand of banana stalk fiber from the mouth of an allegedly bewitched patient. . . ."

The doctors, Ramon R. Angeles and Ernesto Brion of the National Bureau of Investigation (NBI), did not try to explain what they saw. They merely recommended prosecution. Later in the story they were quoted as believing that the "miracle cures were nothing more than medical quackery based on mass hypnotism and religious faith."

In 1959 Tony Agpaoa had been charged with practicing medicine illegally and fined. In the *Daily Mirror* dated August 1, 1959, the following story was most likely the reason that attention was drawn to the young healer. Certainly the PMA did not enjoy having this story published in a major newspaper:

A 22-year-old miracle healer whose "miraculous powers" consist of performing "successful operations" with his bare hands has certain residents of Sta. Cruz district agog and several ranking Manila police officers believing in him.

The youth's presence in the city was revealed this morning by Capt. José Rarang, chief of the MPD arson section, who turned in a report to Detective Major Enrique Morales.

Rarang identified the healer as Antonio Agpaoa, native of Rosales, Pangasinan. He was unavailable for interview, having left the other day for his hometown.

According to Rarang, the youth performed a successful operation on Det. Conrado Concepcion, in which the latter's peptic ulcers were "removed." Rarang said the operation was carried out July 24.

The other patient cured was Catalina de Leon, 47, of 2126 Anacleto, Sta. Cruz, whose kidney ailment was corrected by the youth on July 27.

Aside from himself, Rarang said, those who witnessed the operation on de Leon were Lt. Pedro Junio, Sgt. Timothy Mercado, Det. Pablo Victorino, Cpl. Nemesio Ilagan, two unidentified professional doctors, and five similarly unnamed ladies.

Describing the operation performed on de Leon by Agpaoa, with the witnesses just three feet away, Rarang said the youth, after baring the stomach of the woman, made a sign with his hands as if to inflict a "cut" at the stomach center.

Rarang said that he and the other witnesses were surprised when they saw blood spurt at the place where the youth made the sign. Then the healer inserted two fingers inside the wound and brought out the intestines.

Both operations were performed in the residence of Det. Concepcion at 2593 Kalimbas, Sta. Cruz.

Rarang said he will be the next patient of the youth upon the latter's return to the city. Rarang was supposed to have been operated upon yesterday. The arson chief did not say what kind of ailment he has.

Two months later, in October, Tony became the first healer to be indicted under the newly enacted Medical Act of 1959. He was found guilty and fined 1,000 pesos, about $100. The witnesses included Detective Concepcion. There was no doubt that Tony had practiced medicine without passing the medical examinations or possessing a license. However, he was not charged with fraud.

The newspaper account of Tony's arrest is intriguing:

Two detectives walked into the "clinic" of a young faith healer yesterday noon [October 5, 1959] and stopped him from performing another "miracle" on the rheumatic legs of a 65-year-old patient.

Towed to police headquarters by Dets. Ruben Escarcha and Marcel Bonafe was Antonio Agpaoa, who said he comes from Pangasinan.

Agpaoa was massaging the legs of Mrs. Juana Lisedeco, 497 Pavia, Tondo, with a battery-powered massaging device when the detectives came to write finis to his faith healing days.

At police headquarters, where some of his patients and the usual bunch of curious had followed him, Agpaoa gave a four-page statement about his activities. His counsel, Wencesiao Laureta, allowed him to sign the statement following a brief consultation in Ilocano.

Charged with illegal practice of medicine, Agpaoa was released after posting a P1,000 bond.

Taken from his "clinic," at 1403 Ibarra, Sampaloc, were several notebooks with the names and addresses of his patients, an electric massager, a pair of surgical tweezers, a bottle of alcohol, some cotton balls, adhesive tape, gauze, and urine specimens.

José S. Santos, 70, a retired mechanic of the Alabang serum and vaccine laboratories, offered to tell the police how Agpaoa had, with his bare hands, "successfully" operated on his ulcers only last Wednesday.

Among Agpaoa's papers was the original and a photostatic memoran-
dum allegedly signed by a Malacanang aide asking authorities not to
molest Agpaoa.

Agpaoa, the eldest of six children of Moises Agpaoa and Felicidad
Contreras of Rosales, Pangasinan, said the "power to heal" came upon
him when he was nine, when he suddenly recovered from a serious case
of mumps. He said he has been going around curing people ever since,
calling on his "divine powers" before and after operating on a patient.

Not a word about fakery appears in the story, and nothing
indicating the paraphernalia necessary to fake psychic surgery
was listed among the confiscated items. A major Filipino prejudice also stands out because of the pointed mention that Tony
spoke to his attorney in Ilocano, a dialect looked down upon
by the majority of Filipinos, who speak Tagalog. Also of
special interest was the account of Tony's acquiring the "power
to heal." There are a number of versions to this same story.
The "mumps" story was new to me.

The newspapers were filled with stories about various spontaneous "miracles" similar to the famous Lady of Lourdes,
France, but on a smaller scale. For example, Dalmacio Mico,
sixty, drew huge crowds to his rice paddy near San Fernando
in summer of 1956. One account said that he placed a crow-
bar in a black rock, and water came out. He drank some water,
and he became a healer. The accounts of spontaneous miracles
listed a number of claimed cures, such as: "The blind could
see; the crippled could walk. Cancer, diabetes, ulcers—all were
cured." In one account a female healer, Vilma Mendoza, sev-
enteen, of Naawan, drew such large crowds that the authorities feared an epidemic due to the filthy, crowded conditions.
When they tried to shut her down, the people rioted and
threatened officials with bodily harm.

Philippine authorities are justifiably angry at the epidemics
caused by the crowded conditions that exist when thousands
of peasants flock to a "miracle" scene or person. The terrible
conditions kill more people than the miracles can possibly save.

In one case sixty natives drowned when an overcrowded ferry taking passengers to an island to a healer capsized.

Adding to the problems that Tony and the members of the Espiritistas face from the government are cases such as this one, from April, 1972: "Self-proclaimed healer Romulo DeAngel, 29, was charged in the death of Alfredo Catumbre, a 'patient' who sustained nail hole bleedings 400 times."

We spent an entire day reading clips in the *Manila Times* morgue, and I noted that the Filipino Board of Medical Examiners had argued the merits of acupuncture back in 1963 and concluded that it had no value. I wonder if that attitude has changed in conjunction with the change in the United States?

When a young engineer goes into industry, he quickly distinguishes two separate worlds. On the one hand, the laboratory, with its well defined laws governing experiments that can be repeated and the image it presents of a comprehensible world. On the other hand there is the "real" universe, where laws do not always apply, and where events cannot always be foreseen, or impossible things happen.

Jacques Bergier and Louis Pauwels
Morning of the Magicians

4 Firsthand View of Surgery

BAGUIO CITY is like Monterey, California, with its pine-covered mountains, cool breezes, abundant flora, and stately hillside homes. Tony Agpaoa's home and chapel are constructed together in an attractive split-level house built into the steep side of a mountain. There is no access drive from Kennon Road to Tony's house, so visitors must clamor down a partially paved path on foot. It is said that many a remarkable healing has been dramatically proclaimed when a formerly crippled patient strolls back up the 400 feet of steep incline.

When Marlyn and I arrived at the Agpaoa residence to see psychic surgeries performed on members of our tour, the rainy season was still about two weeks away, and climatic conditions were ideal. The magnificent scenery, the perfect weather, the amiable people, and the anticipation of seeing the phenomenon for the first time made this particular Saturday morning unforgettable.

Tony and his family live on the upper level of the large house; the main level is comprised of guest rooms, a living room, a dining room, and an "observation room." The latter is a viewing station in which visitors may look down through an opening to the lower level operating room. We watched our first live showing of psychic surgery from this vantage point.

The first patient of the morning was Dorothy Bequette, a Filipino-American from San José, California. This was her second visit to Tony for healing within a year's time. She joined our tour shortly after being informed by her physician that she required surgery to remove a massive benign tumor in her abdomen. Dorothy was lying face up on the operating table.

As Dorothy awaited the healer, I looked at her thin body and recalled that most detractors argue that the healers always choose an obese patient in order to make it appear as if the fingers enter the body when they merely sink their hands into the folds of the flesh. There wasn't an ounce of excess fat on

Dorothy Bequette. In fact, her illness had caused a major loss of weight.

Tony said a brief prayer while he stood over the patient; then he looked up at the gallery of curious and excited onlookers, smiled broadly, and showed us there was nothing hidden in the palms of his hands. He then placed one hand on Dorothy's forehead and the other on her stomach.

I noted the positions of the other persons in the operating room. Jane Waddington, one of Rosita's students who made the trip to become ordained into Tony's church, was his first assistant. He was assisted also by two Filipino boys. I watched the two boys like a hawk as Tony was making his preparations, but I detected nothing suspicious in their actions. Standing next to the table to view the surgery from close range was Ms. Grace Moore, a registered nurse from San José who was on the tour expressly to "see this thing for myself."

Just before his fingers dug into Dorothy's flesh and opened her body, Tony lifted a small wad of water-soaked cotton from a plastic basin held by Jane Waddington. Clear water ran over Dorothy's belly as Tony's fingers worked in a rapid, smooth kneading motion. At first watery blood and finally dark blood gurgled from between his fingers. Dorothy's face showed that she was fully conscious. She looked up at me and winked; obviously she felt no pain. Tony suddenly stopped the kneading motion and parted the skin and muscle. The entire procedure was practically bloodless. He glanced up at our gallery and smiled, holding the flesh wide open for a full minute as shutters snapped and flashbulbs exploded. I could not see any intestine. The skin and some layers of subcutaneous flesh were parted.

Tony then went to work. The show was over, and he was intent on his business as his hands kneaded and probed inside Dorothy's abdomen. In a few seconds he lifted a large mass of pulpy, bloody tissue out of the opening with his right hand and brandished it for all to see before he placed it into a container of formaldehyde so that Dorothy could take it home. He kneaded her flesh a while longer; then he prepared us for the closing. If the opening was dramatic, the closing was amazing. Faster than the eye can follow, practically undetectable on slow motion film, what appeared to be an open wound vanished without a trace.

"Wow, wasn't that something to see?" exclaimed a woman standing next to me. I didn't mean to sound abrupt or hurt her feelings, but I was all business at the time. I replied:

"I really can't say. We're fifteen feet away standing up here, and I simply can't be certain that what I saw was real."

I decided I wanted to be in the operating room, right next to the table, for the next operation.

After surgery Tony explained to the gathering that he had removed a great deal of physical matter from Dorothy's body; therefore it was necessary for him to balance the "yin and yang." He explained that Chinese acupuncture and psychic surgery are medical cousins. He said that he used a subtle form of acupuncture to anesthetize the area when he performed operations. Then he stepped to the foot of the table and placed his thumbs between Dorothy's large and second toes. He pressed, without effort, and she arched her body, obviously in pain.

"It felt like a thousand volts of electricity running through me," she said afterward.

"When he did it to me," commented Gary Davidson, also from San José, "it felt like a hacksaw digging into me."

I felt that the toe-pushing treatment was intended as much for the viewers' benefit as it was for Dorothy's balance. It's a common yoga technique to rub the toes and between them for relaxation, and it requires no psychic ability to make it hurt by pressuring there.

When Dorothy got off the table, I moved downstairs and took a station next to Ms. Moore, the nurse, and Bill Heim, a Chicago industrialist who was filming the operations. A fifteen-year-old boy from Brookfield, Illinois, was getting onto the table. Mike Jablonski, tall and extremely thin, is a muscular dystrophy victim. He had made this trip with his mother, Candida Jablonski, in hopes of stemming the disease that threatened to reduce him to a vegetable.

As Tony ran his hands over the young man's torso, I watched his assistants. I could detect nothing amiss; if they were hiding pieces of tissue and tiny containers of blood, they were fantastically adroit. It was a cinch that Tony had nothing in his hands—or up his short-sleeved shirt.

Tony said he would not open the Jablonski boy's body at this time, but he did give the youngster some of the yin and yang toe treatment.

Later Mike agreed with Davidson: "It felt more like a hacksaw cutting than it did electricity."

The next patient was a woman in her late sixties. She joined the tour because she hoped to get help for a vision problem. She had a sinus problem as well, and Tony indicated that he was going to operate on her nose. She was seated on a stool instead of the operating table. Nose polyps are a favorite with Tony—they are also alleged by many detractors to be easily faked.

She seated herself, closed her eyes, and awaited the miracle-making fingers of the surgeon. Tony again dipped into the basin and brought out the saturated cotton wad. Again his fingers worked, and water flowed, followed by watery blood and dark blood. This is a natural progression: the watery cotton dribbles unmixed water at first; then a little blood mixes in; finally blood runs freely. The color of the darkest blood flowing from the woman was lighter in color than the blood that flowed from Dorothy Bequette's abdomen. Either the blood fakers are clever enough to vary their props, or the genuine difference in the blood color was appearing.

Breathing through her mouth, the woman tilted her head back as blood ran down the sides of her face. Unlike the situation in most of the operations that I had viewed on film, the blood did not flow into her mouth. I had already concluded that if this type surgery were genuine, there would necessarily be some blood entering the patient's throat. When blood ran into the patient's mouth from the outside, this hypothesis was negated. After two pulpy tissue masses alleged to be polyps had been removed, the patient nearly choked on blood in her throat and had to spit it out. Since it was impossible for me to tell if the operation was genuine on the basis of observation alone, I concluded it to be genuine on the basis of the blood in her throat.

There was a pause in the action and some clamor between patients, so I used the opportunity to question Grace Moore. Since she had been only a few feet away from the action and was a registered nurse, I valued her opinion:

"Well, it really doesn't look real. I mean it doesn't look like orthodox surgery—but, then, I guess it isn't anything like orthodox surgery, so maybe we shouldn't expect it to look the same. As far as I can tell, his fingers go inside the body to the peritoneal membrane, but he doesn't penetrate it. I did not see blood spurt from the veins, and I didn't see any intestine or organs."

Tony's next patient was Elmer Mitchell, fifty-three, of Fairfax, Missouri. Mitchell had suffered severe back pains ever since a tractor accident mashed several vertebrae back in 1957. The farmer scrambled onto the table, sprawled face down, and waited for the healer. As Tony ran his fingers up and down Mitchell's spine, I inched closer. I was standing behind the healer; from this position I could observe his palms as he worked. Tony paused, looked up at the gallery, and explained how he anesthetized by touching various acupuncture points with his fingertips.

Agpaoa indicated that he was going to open Mitchell at a point on the back of his neck near the base of his skull. The cotton wad was dropped into the basin of clear tap water (I had watched as one of the assistants filled the basin). Peering into the basin, I checked the cotton; were anything artificial enclosed in the cotton, it would have shown up clearly in the transparency of the saturated material. The cotton was clean. Tony grinned at me and my efforts:

"Nothing in cotton, Tom," he said, greatly amused.

He followed the same procedure as before—the movement of

his fingers caused clear water to run over the patient's neck. This time I could see the cotton in his hands. The red, bloody substance saturated the cotton from the bottom up.

Tony worked on Mitchell's neck for a few seconds; then he suddenly spread his fingers a few inches apart to reveal the opening. Perhaps I should have been able to see white bone and arteries spurting blood, but I did not. I saw only fleshy pink tissue and very little blood. Two round globs of yellowish tissue were plainly visible in the opening. On distance-perception tests I've always done well, and it appeared to me that the globs of tissue were below the skin level, indicating that Tony was indeed working inside the body. I was not invited to test the opening with my finger, and I did not ask.

Jane Waddington, instructed by Tony, plucked the globs of tissue from Mitchell's neck with a pair of forceps. Mitchell told me later that he felt something going on down inside his neck, but it didn't hurt. Again I was forced to conclude that sight alone was not proof of the body openings. This may sound ultraconservative to many, but I was not about to risk having suggestion delude my objectivity. If I were seeing the insides of people, I preferred to leave no doubt. As the next patient, Wes McEwen, of Port Angeles, Washington, said:

"Guts are guts, and bones are bones. I've seen plenty of both and the insides of a lot of soldiers who got shot up, and it never looked like this."

Four persons present that morning, Marlyn, Wes, Grace Moore, and I, agreed that the openings did not *look* real; but on the other hand there had been no detectable fakery, and circumstances other than vision attested to the validity of the openings.

Wes "Mac" McEwen had fought his way from Manila to this same Baguio back in 1942. He is the victim of a hereditary condition best described as spinal muscular atrophy. He had trouble walking, his hands were numb, and he was losing his sense of touch and coordination as well as his strength. In fact, he was losing everything except his sense of humor. Like Mitchell before him, Wes crawled onto the table and lay belly down.

Again Tony ran his hands over the bare back and plucked cotton from the basin. Again I checked the cotton, the towels, and the sheet that covered him. Again the healer's palms were clearly visible as his hands descended on the back of Wes McEwen's neck. This time very little blood ran, and Tony wasted no time before parting the flesh. This time I leaned in even closer to the action and peered between Tony's fingers into what certainly appeared to be a deep opening in the patient's neck. Again I saw no bone or arteries, but Tony exposed some muscle tissue and told Jane Waddington to pull it out with the forceps.

Then something remarkable occurred.

As Jane tugged on the tissue, it snapped and shredded at the end, but it didn't budge. From a few inches away I could see plainly that the material, resembling the subcutaneous flesh most cooks rip out of chicken when they prepare it, was not held in place by Tony's fingers. Yet it didn't slip out of Mac's body easily.

Tony urged, "Take it. Take it," and Jane tried again. Again it shredded without coming out. Finally on the third try a stringy piece of tissue, about four inches long and an inch wide, slithered out of the opening and dangled from the forceps. Tony made a cursory examination of the wound and let it close.

It was evidently a harrowing experience for Tony because he called time for a break. Wes and I chatted about the operation:

"Had a little trouble with this tough old bird, didn't he?"

"I guess so. What did it feel like?" I replied.

"Whatever was going on was going on down inside my neck. I know that much."

Wes McEwen could look on with detached objectivity; he was neither a believer nor a nonbeliever. He was an interested observer, and even though he had a serious condition requiring the healer's help, he refused to be psyched by the unusual happenings.

About twenty-five people were mingling and chattering over hot coffee and cakes when I climbed to the top of the stairs.

Tony was nowhere in sight. I started to take a cookie and pour a cup of coffee when Marlyn rushed out and told me to hurry into the back bedroom. Tony was about to operate on Marla Kelly, a twenty-four-year-old woman from Los Angeles.

Marla was a headache victim. She had sustained severe pain for several years, and physicians were unable to diagnose, let alone solve, the problem. When we reached the bedroom, Tony was talking to the spectators. Then he turned to put his hands on Marla's head. I stepped back to snap pictures, and Marlyn stepped up for a close look. Tony wet Marla's forehead, but he tossed the cotton away instead of keeping it in his hand. When he opened her forehead, he simply jammed the tip of his finger in. Marlyn saw the white flash of bone before blood covered it up.

Blood flowed freely down Marla's face as Tony pinched around with his fingertips and removed a small, burrlike object. The operation was brief. Marla had felt no pain, but a few days later she complained that the headaches continued. They stayed with her for the rest of the week, and they were ultimately eliminated by another healer.

John and Millie Hall, of Lincolnwood, Illinois, had joined us on the tour. The Halls are personal friends who came along to witness the phenomenon, not necessarily for healing. However, both Millie and John had psychic operations, and I watched both at close range in the same back bedroom of the main level in Tony's home.

John had casually mentioned to Tony that he was hard of hearing in one of his ears, but he wasn't sure which. Tony cupped his hands and held them up near the side of John's head with the palms aimed inward at the ears.

"I suddenly felt a ringing in my left ear; Tony grinned and said, 'The left one.'"

Before he opened John Hall's body, Tony massaged the back of John's ear for several minutes. He seemed to be deep in thought as he peered out the window and let his fingers massage without his conscious guidance. Finally he swabbed behind John's ear with water and parted the flesh. He removed two small, gristlelike lumps, held them a moment, and tossed them into a wastebasket. Then he closed the area.

Rosita entered the room and watched as Tony ran his fingers around the area he had just opened and closed. I chose that time to question the need for the watery cotton. Rosita answered for Tony; in fact, whenever Rosita was in Tony's company and I asked questions, she took the initiative to answer for him. Tony agreed with her reply:

"Sometimes the healers use water because it is a life force, and other times they use fire for the same purpose. There are hundreds of ways healers can operate."

As Rosita explained, Tony moved quietly over to Millie Hall and looked at her eyes. Millie's eyelids were dotted with sebaceous cysts. Tony indicated that he would remove them. When he operated, it appeared simple enough: he fingered her eyes, rolled the eyelids back, and lifted out some tiny pieces of tissue.

If he's faking, I mused to myself, he's a miracle magician. Being able to juggle corresponding parts of tissue from room to room and operation to operation in order to match what he claims he's removing from the body is no mean feat.

In Millie Hall's case there was definite proof that the operation was genuine. Before the surgery she had three small cysts along the edge of each eyelid. She wasn't concerned about those tiny cysts; she was hoping, however, that Tony would eliminate the larger cysts near the center and upper rim of the eyelid. When Tony finished, Millie touched her eyes and complained that nothing was done. But the six tiny cysts were gone, and they have not reappeared as of this writing.

During the mid-morning Tony seemed tireless. He galloped down the stairs to the operating room after working on fifteen-year-old Kathi Hall, John and Millie's granddaughter, who had a serious case of acne on her back. I ran along behind him and watched as he worked on seventy-four-year-old Alexander Klahre, of Forks, Washington.

The elderly man had a serious circulation problem, which caused his feet and ankles to swell badly. He also had a spinal problem and was unable to walk without support from a walker. Tony removed some stringy tissue from the small of Mr. Klahre's back in a quick operation involving a tiny incision. When Tony finished, Jane Waddington guided Klahre by the hands, arms outstretched, and coaxed him to walk without support. He managed to stride out of the operating room, and the onlookers cheered. I didn't want to spoil the festivities, so I kept quiet about feeling that Klahre didn't appear all that improved—at least not at that particular time.

After Klahre left the operating room, everyone returned to the dining area, leaving me alone in the lower level of the house. I took the opportunity to check the small bathroom and a corridor leading from the operating room to the chapel. I checked every nook and cranny for possible stashing places for materials that could be used in fakery. There was no sign of anything suspicious, and I failed to detect any telltale odors. I was convinced that the operations in that house on that morning were not wrought by sleight of hand. We were not hypnotized, and I certainly wasn't allowing myself to be suggestible.

I also explored Tony's chapel, a medium-sized room with brilliantly colored paintings covering the walls and ceiling. The paintings depict Tony's life story. It's impressive but a bit gaudy.

While I was probing around downstairs, Marlyn was trying to locate me. Tony had moved into the back bedroom to operate on Linda McCool, from Saratoga, California, who was visiting the healer in hopes of having scar tissue and screws removed from her spinal column. This case was of particular interest to me, especially coming on the heels of the Mrs. Raymond Steinberg controversy, and I had pointedly asked permission to be present. Tony and Rosita had promised that I would be notified in plenty of time to witness the surgery.

It's possible (but in my opinion unlikely) that it could have been an oversight due to all the morning's activity that Tony forgot my request. Marlyn happened to notice when Tony quietly guided Linda away from the luncheon table. Since Tony had told me he was finished for the day before everyone went upstairs, I wasn't concerned at the time.

By the time Marlyn found me and I had rushed upstairs, Tony had finished. I saw Linda and her companion, Lillian Aherne, also of Saratoga, and asked what happened.

"Tony operated on my back," she said.

"Did he take out the screws?" I asked.

"Yes, he showed them to me."

"Do you have them? I'd like to see them."

"No. I asked for them, but Tony said he needed them for some kind of research or something."

I spotted Rosita and asked her to intercede, to get the screws so that I could photograph them. She went into a bedroom, conferred with Tony, and returned, shrugging.

"Tony says he has already thrown them out. They're gone."

That's all there was to that! An opportunity to provide concrete, irrefutable evidence was thrown away. Only x ray evidence was still available.

Later that afternoon, in the courtyard of the Villa LaMaja, where Tony houses most of his guests, I talked with Linda McCool. I discussed the possibility of the screw removal's being pure hokum. Inadvertently I blabbed about Mrs. Steinberg's hip-plate case, in which Tony's alleged removal had been a hoax. Ms. McCool grew upset, and later I realized my error. It is wrong for one person to intrude into the anxieties of another without being invited.

Many times Tony and his disciples have claimed that the attitude of the patient is as important as the work of the healer in bringing about a total cure. Since this claim has been neither proved nor disproved, I was remiss in disregarding the possibility. Fortunately Linda McCool ignored my statements and maintained confidence in Tony. As of this writing she feels much improved. She says that x rays taken since her return show that the screws have indeed been removed.

Ms. McCool's case represents an excellent testimonial for the authenticity of psychic surgery because she has had seven operations by orthopedic surgeons and is thoroughly familiar with her own back problems.

Of the thirty-five persons on our tour, twenty-four had surgery or treatment of one kind or another. Several of them visited other healers in the vicinity, some with Tony's consent and others without it, and none of the patients have complained as of this writing. Neither my wife nor I sustained any surgery; we tried but were denied. I asked Tony if he would remove my adenoids, but he dodged this request by pointing out that I wasn't ill and therefore didn't need his help.

Tour members later had different comments about their experiences.

Dorothy Bequette was examined by her doctor upon her return, and he was puzzled. The massive tumor he diagnosed earlier had apparently regressed. Dorothy did not tell him of her visit to Baguio. The recommended surgery, so vital to her well-being in early June, was no longer necessary in late June.

Gary Davidson, who had been struck on the head by a baseball bat and sustained brain damage, which caused epileptic seizures, said that his spells are far less frequent and last only a brief time. "There's no foaming and no crossed eyes now," he said, with obvious delight.

Davidson is convinced that he will eventually be totally cured. Our tour was his second visit to the Filipino healers after orthodox medicine gave him up as lost. "I really think the only reason I have any spells at all now is because I'm working with paint remover and other chemicals."

Candida Jablonski reported that Mike "felt better when he first came home, and he still has more energy and vitality than he had before the trip. We're very hopeful he will continue to improve, as Tony said he would."

The woman with the flickering eye problem has been cured, and she believes that her sight is beginning to improve. Her bothersome sinus condition was eliminated the instant she slid off the stool following the operation. At that time she exclaimed, "What do you know? I can breathe! I can actually breathe in fresh air."

John Hall cannot honestly tell if his hearing has improved in the left ear or if it's the result of wishful thinking. Millie Hall voices the only disappointment—she still faces surgery on the larger cysts in her eyelids.

Alexander Klahre had to buy new shoes because the swelling in his feet went down so drastically. However, he still must use his walker to get around.

Elmer Mitchell's back felt the fingertip artistry of three healers—Tony, his former pupil Marcello Jainar, and Placido Palitayan. "All of them did me some good. I'm free of pain for the first time in fifteen years—that's a hell of a lot more than doctors over here could do for me."

Irene Everett, sixty-four, of San José, rode a wheelchair to Baguio, and she walked without it when we returned. Tony removed huge masses of tissue from Ms. Everett, who was seriously overweight; she also suffered from colonitis and diabetes. She feels that the trip was invaluable.

Connie Johnston, Klahre's daughter, was unimpressed with Tony's operation on her gall bladder. X rays taken in mid-July showed that the stones were still present. However, she reported, "I haven't had any symptoms since the healings. I'm not going to do anything about those stones as long as I feel fine."

Dr. Kurt Osolsobie, an Austrian psychologist, was unimpressed by Agpaoa, also because of an alleged gallstone operation.

"It was a fake—the operation on my gallstones," he said.

Osolsobie didn't wait long before checking up on Tony's claims. Three days after the operation, during which Tony showed him some "fleshy stuff that didn't look at all like gallstones," he had x rays taken at the Notre Dame Hospital in Baguio. The original stones were still present.

"I suspected as much when it didn't feel to me as if his hands went inside, and the blood that ran on my stomach was cool," Osolsobie said of his operation. He confronted Tony with the x ray. "He drained of color—turned white as a sheet; then later, when he regained his composure, he suggested some magnetic treatments to make the stones disappear."

Osolsobie's operation was performed with only his wife, Heidi, and one of Tony's assistants present. "Heidi thought the operation looked phony, and she thinks the whole phenomenon is phony, but I'm not ready to condemn it on the basis of what I've experienced here."

Many of the other people with us in Baguio were impressed more by other healers than they were by Tony. Many investigators have returned with glowing reports of the others and little good to say about Tony. However, Agpaoa is the healer with the most widely known name and reputation. He is the one Filipino mystic with enough sophistication to attract Americans and Europeans. His is also the most controversial personality.

I had heard many reports about Tony, and the testimony was conflicting. To some Tony had a "mystic presence, which was both soothing and awesome at the same time." One man said: "He's truly a man of God," while another saw him as a "jolly, smiling, wonderful little man who loves life and people." Yet there were others who saw Tony as "a scoundrel, a money-grabbing fraud with no regard for anyone."

Comments about Lucy were equally diffuse and contrasting.

"She's a clever businesswoman. She leaves Tony alone and runs her business. There's nothing wrong with that," stated one former visitor. Another claimed, "Lucy's a jewel. She sacrifices for the sake of Tony. Think of what she must go through never getting any time alone with her husband and having all those other people adore him." One American woman, who obviously became a victim of the doctor-patient love syndrome and fell for Tony in a big way, had this to say:

"Lucy is a witch. She's a jealous witch who puts deadly hexes on people."

On three different occasions, taxi drivers who know the Agpaoas told us, "Lucy is Tony's evil genius; she has caused his tragic downfall."

When we arrived in Baguio, it didn't seem to us that Tony had suffered much of a "tragic downfall." Nevertheless a number of Filipinos told me they were certain he had debased his "gift"; they thought that by commercializing his ability he is courting the wrath of God.

With many conflicting opinions ricocheting around in my head, I determined that the personalities were to be viewed as objectively as the phenomenon. They are an integral part of the total study of psychic surgery. We first met Lucy in Chicago at Rosita's home. Lucy is quiet; she understands English, but she does not speak it well. She's self-assured and competent. In America Lucy would be hailed as a shrewd businesswoman. In the Philippines, as the wife of a spiritual healer and religious leader, she is considered greedy by many. From what I observed, I do not buy the thesis that Lucy is responsible for Tony's "downfall." We are not certain Tony is headed for *any* spiritual downfall. He's quite inconsistent, yes, but that does not indicate that he's losing his healing ability.

I met Tony Agpaoa the first evening we were in Baguio. He came to chat with his guests, and I'm sure he was fully aware of my presence and my intentions. When he entered the room, I did not detect any special "presence"; rather, I felt he was a little introverted. I watched him from a distance of about twenty feet. He is a dapper dresser and a polished, congenial host—a far cry from the other healers, who are dirt farmers with no sophistication to appeal to American or European visitors. Wes McEwen wrote in his daily logbook this impression of Tony:

"He's a small, quiet, smiling man—seems deep in thought, and he listens more than he talks."

For a number of years Tony has been absorbing information and culture from his guests. He has accumulated a great amount of medical knowledge over a period of a few years. His knowledge of nutrition, anatomy, physiology, and psychology is remarkable, especially for a third grade dropout.

I approached Tony and extended my hand. He knew me without introduction and said simply, "How are you, Tom?" His hand was indeed tiny and soft, as Joe Pyne had noted. He did not exude any exceptional charisma. At that moment in my company he was ill at ease and seemed a bit defensive. Surely he and Rosita had huddled to contemplate this journalist and his book, of which neither of them especially approved. Besides, I was neither a believer nor a skeptic, and the most difficult type of person for healers to cope with are analytical souls who become neither involved and impressed nor loudly skeptical. The believer is a delight for the healer. Many times Tony beamed his pleasure when the others responded with exclamations of wonder. Skeptics can be ignored or even laughed at as "poor fellows who simply don't understand." However, the detached analyst neither exclaims nor sneers; he watches intently and bothers the healer with questions.

By any standards the Agpaoas are a wealthy family. His home is large and impressive. He owns a nightclub in Baguio and is on the board of directors of the cockfights—traditionally a lucrative endeavor in the Philippines. Lucy and he own the Diplomat Tours enterprise, which includes a touring car garage service, and Lucy owns a dress shop and hairstyle parlor. I noted that most of the women on our tour purchased handmade pants suits from Lucy, which cost $80 or more. The rate of currency exchange while we were there was $1 for P6.70. (Agpaoa employees granted a flat exchange rate of P6.00.) Tony drives a new Mustang and is obviously a powerful and influential man in Baguio City. The chamber of commerce must love him, even if they don't believe, because of the great number of tourists he attracts.

All of Tony's material gains come directly from his healing ability and his wife's business sense. Some of the other healers are overtly envious. I took their statements with a grain of salt when they pointed at Tony's commercialization of the "gift" with one hand and held the other out for a donation in greenbacks.

However, one healer, whom I met only briefly, did not deride Agpaoa. Brother David Oligani, a healer who refuses even donations to his church, shed genuine tears when he contemplated "brother Tony." All he would say was, "I do not understand brother Tony." In the eyes of this practicing man of God, who exemplified his beliefs with humility, charity, and austerity, Tony Agpaoa has committed sacrilege. But, true to his philosophy, Oligani does not condemn Tony; nor does he add to the cross he believes Tony must bear. Oligani is content to let the universe deal with the problem without chipping in his two bits' worth of negativity.

One of Tony's former patients who has become disenchanted and distressed at news that Tony is charging a fee for his healing had this to say: "Jesus Christ would not have charged for a miracle; I don't see why Tony Agpaoa should do so."

Regardless of what his devoted followers may believe, Tony is not in the same class with Christ, so the comparison is totally invalid. The matter of a fee has absolutely no relevance to the phenomenon, but it is part of the controversy surrounding Tony and must be considered.

It is the AMA's contention that quacks, which include psychic surgeons, do damage in two respects: one, quackery deprives many persons of needed orthodox medical treatment; and two, it bilks them out of money.

Since most of Tony's patients have been to many physicians before giving up as "incurables," the first allegation does not stand up. As for individuals being bilked, one need only read the testimonials cited by Senator Edward Kennedy in his national health proposals to see what orthodox medicine can cost and to realize that Tony is far from unique.

Yet though we may dismiss the AMA's allegations, we cannot dismiss the philosophical implications of charging a fee for performing God's work. According to Rosita, it is against Tony's philosophy to charge a fee; he can accept donations but cannot charge a fee. On our tour there was no report of fee-charging. Tony's employees handed out envelopes for donations to his church and to Marcello's church. Tony's father, Moises, charged several tour members for massages. According to several guests, he charged $15. It has been said that Tony disciplines his father for this practice, but evidently it doesn't phase the man.

Some women have complained that when Moises gives a massage, he gets a bit carried away. However, no one has yet accused Moises of being a man of God and leader of a church.

Despite the philosophical conflict of interest, there have been documented instances in which Agpaoa levied a definite fee for his psychic surgery. Evidently it has not been the rule but the exception in past years.

Laurette Dempsey, of Highland Park, Illinois, tells of being charged a fee for Tony's services. Her husband, Al, died of cancer in June, 1972, after he underwent psychic surgery by Tony in May of the same year. Ms. Dempsey is not resentful. She said, "We gave Tony $1,000, and it would have been worth more. Tony did help my husband; he was able to sleep and eat, and the pain was considerably lessened. People with us on the trip noticed his improvement. His last days were better because of Tony."

When they arrived in Baguio, Laurette Dempsey asked Tony if her husband would live. Tony replied, "Of course, he will live." He didn't say for how long, however. Tony performed one operation on Dempsey right away, but he explained that the further necessary operations would cost $1,000 and Tony needed to travel to Manila for "some black market medicine. The cost will be $150."

Three days later Tony showed up with the medicine, which was never defined or explained. Laurette Dempsey gave this description:

"When Tony started, he shot some stuff into Al with five huge hypodermic needles; then he opened him up with his hands. Tony told me that subsequent operations would cost $800. I wrote him a check and was happy because Al was able to eat without pain immediately after the first operation."

Later, Ms. Dempsey wrote to Tony, asking for a receipt from his church for the money. In a letter dated June 13, 1972, Tony wrote back to say, "Sorry, but I cannot issue you a receipt for the donation you gave for the church." He did not explain his reason.

Others who were charged a fee unexpectedly were not so gracious as Laurette Dempsey. Tony's inconsistency in matters of money doesn't help the reputation of psychic surgeons. Some of the persons who join Tony's tourist trade don't help the reputation much, either.

In Mexico City, at the time of this writing, Diplomat Tours arranged for an exclusive representation through a travel agency, which insists that travelers must make a "payment in advance" for surgery. According to Margarita Velasco, whom we met in Baguio City, the rates are $300 for three operations and anywhere from $50 to $500 for additional surgery. Perhaps Tony isn't aware of such goings on, but it is doubtful.

There are two points of view regarding money and psychic surgery—one modern and materialistic, the other severely austere.

Many people feel that regardless of how the phenomenon is worked, Tony and the other healers must put in their time as the instruments. Therefore they are entitled to just compensation.

Brother Oligani is perhaps the greatest example of the other viewpoint. He makes about P3,000 per year as a rice farmer. He gets up at 4:00 A.M. daily and rides a carabao to his fields, where he toils until the sun gets too hot. Then he returns to his chapel and heals the sick. He accepts no donations from them.

"He has chased after people to give them back a few centavos they left in his chapel," one patient said.

Oligani built his facilities with his own hard-earned funds. He dresses poorly, and he dresses his children poorly. He spends nothing on himself, but he gives freely to others.

It would seem that Oligani is truly a man of God, but part of his philosophy is inconsistent with the apparent laws of the universe. When a person is cured by a healer or a doctor, it is only natural for that person to want to pay for the services rendered. If there is one universal law to which we can all attest, it is the law that "you don't get something for nothing." Brother David, as well-meaning as he is, may be creating a burden for his patients by not allowing them to repay him by contributing to his church.

As a healer Oligani ranks with Juan Blanche, who is considered by many to be more phenomenal than Agpaoa. Indeed, there are many healers with ability equal to Tony's; what they lack is his personality.

Placido is one of Baguio's healers who would love to emulate Tony's success. We were directed to Placido by a taxi driver, Saturnino David, who was formerly one of Tony's assistants. He said he had a falling out with Lucy over money, and he blamed Lucy for Tony's inconsistency. But he did not go into detail. David introduced us to Placido, and later we learned that Placido often shared his "donations" with cabbies who brought him American tourists.

Placido was the healer being considered for transport to the United States as part of the Dreyfus Foundation plans at that time. He is a tiny man, less than five feet tall and lighter than ninety pounds. He's fidgety and high strung. The night we met he promised to work on Marlyn later in the week. Marlyn made an ideal test patient because she had a number of well-diagnosed minor problems that would be easily verified were a healer to improve the condition. For example, she had a hiatal hernia near her diaphragm in which she can feel the bubble-like fissure. The hernia had been there since she was six years old. It didn't bother her, but were a healer to close it, the evidence would be impressive. Placido never did operate on Marlyn; he backed down nervously each time we met.

David explained that Dr. Kurt Osolsobie and I as a team made Placido extremely nervous and unable to work. This is understandable. I even felt a twinge of sympathy for Placido when Marlyn appeared for her initial "diagnosis and operation." She was wearing a bikini under her clothing in order to negate the need for the usual sheet or blanket. We were trying to control the conditions as much as possible. The look on poor Placido's face when Marlyn stepped out of her skirt and displayed the bikini was one of pure astonishment. Marlyn lay face up on the crude wooden table inside Placido's dank gray cement chapel, and he concentrated on her. His diagnosis was impressive. He called the hernia a "small fracture in mid-chest"; he pointed to a spot on her back and said it hurt, which was correct; and he noted she had a slight nervous flutter in her heartbeat, which is also correct (Marlyn has a tiny valve leakage). He tried to meditate and operate but then postponed the operation. He was visibly upset.

Placido performed only one surgery while Dr. Osolsobie and I were looking on. The abdominal surgery was on a rather obese Filipino woman. The operation was relatively unimpressive as psychic surgeries go, but I don't think it was faked. We have since learned that that patient has had the same piece of tissue removed several times. She appeared as Placido's patient in films brought back by other members of the tour—same girl, same place, same operation, different time.

However, other members of our tour group gave Placido a high recommendation. Evidently if the patient doesn't make him nervous, he performs remarkable surgery.

Herb and Connie Johnston visited Placido after Connie underwent gall bladder surgery performed by Tony. Placido operated to relax a "tightness" in her chest caused by adhesions due to breast surgery earlier that year.

"When Placido opened my chest, there was a sharp snapping sound, like a dry twig breaking. He removed some blood clots and tissue. He said my gall bladder operation by Tony was okay." Ms. Johnston had been concerned about Tony's work ever since he refused to give her the "stones" he removed. "They just didn't look right to me; they looked like little black peas, three or four in a pearl-like string."

Herb and Connie Johnston watched when Placido operated on Candida Jablonski, and after viewing several of Tony's operations, they were far more impressed with what they saw at Placido's chapel.

"His hand sank deep into her abdomen. It was halfway past the back of his hand when he was sloshing around inside her."

Placido removed a small growth from Ms. Jablonski's uterus, and the operation solved a menopause difficulty.

On young Mike Jablonski, the muscular dystrophy victim, Placido operated in a number of places, and each time there was, according to Mike, a "loud snapping sound when he entered. I felt the stuff come from the inside out when he removed the tissue. He didn't use any cotton and water, either. When he opened my chest, it felt as if he was separating or pulling apart the molecules of my skin. There was no pain, just pressure."

Elmer Mitchell also noted the snapping sound made when Placido entered the body. Mitchell compared the three healers who operated on his back. "Tony caused a pressure, sort of like knuckles against my back; Placido seemed to slip inside with ease after the snapping sound, and Marcello pinched."

We heard no snapping sound when Placido operated on his demonstrator model. As for Marcello Jainar, a healer who formerly assisted Tony on a regular basis but who now has his own chapel, we also provided him ample opportunity to demonstrate his ability. Marlyn has definitely diagnosed varicose veins in her legs, and varicose veins are said to be Marcello's specialty. He rubbed Marlyn's legs, but he did not operate. He did not give a reason for the refusal. On the other hand, Myrtle Heim testifies that Marcello "opened my legs wide and stripped the veins as if it were nothing."

The most astonishing operations Marlyn and I witnessed were performed not in Baguio but down in the Pangasinan lowlands near the village where Tony was born. The healer there was José Mercado, and the performances were sensational if, medically speaking, of questionable value.

Mercado is a member of the Espiritistas, and his patients wade through ritual and preaching before operation time. It was in his crowded chapel that we encountered the curious phenomenon of "spiritual injection."

The end of the preaching signaled "injection time" to the more than a hundred persons in the crude, steamy chapel. Those who wanted injections lined up along a wall, and Mercado went to work. It looked like a vaccination line in the navy: the people took turns stepping up so that Mercado could point his finger at them; then they walked away rubbing themselves as if they had been jabbed with a hypodermic needle.

I got in line behind Jack Netchin. When Jack's turn arrived, he was given a hearty jolt that drew blood.

"That felt just like a needle," he exclaimed.

My turn arrived, and my left shoulder was the target. Mercado, grinning from ear to ear, pointed his right forefinger at my upper arm. There was nothing in his hand and nothing protruding from the tip of his finger, yet when he made a slight jerking motion with his hand, I felt a distinct needle jab. A tiny welt and a droplet of blood appeared on the spot.

Diagnosis follows injection time. Those who are ill line up, and Mercado guides them to a sheet held up by his aides. He peers through them, apparently, and occasionally he will startle a Filipino girl by telling her the color of her undergarments.

The first of Mercado's two exceptional surgeries was performed on skeptical Kurt Osolsobie. Kurt had lined up with the sick to go through diagnosis. To his surprise Mercado registered some alarm as he peered into the body of the Viennese psychologist.

"You've had operation. Who did it?" Mercado asked.

"Tony, about five days ago," was the short reply.

Mercado said something in his native dialect, and there was a general buzzing of excitement as the healer hurried Kurt to the large, crudely built wooden table. "Infection," Mercado said. "Bad operation."

Kurt unbuckled his belt and lowered his trousers. He appeared both amused and confused as he complied with Mercado's instructions. Wasting little time, Mercado touched Kurt's flat abdomen; then he snatched a wad of dry cotton from his aide and punched his fingers into Kurt's body. There was a definite "whooshing" sound as he entered. He kneaded briefly with his fingers. Then, with a loud exclamation of "Infection. See?" he squiggled a large glob of pus across Kurt's belly and flipped it to the floor with a flick of his wrist. "Infection," he shouted again, appearing entranced as he worked, and he gouged into Kurt for more of the feculent matter. It certainly looked like pus, and there was a foul odor present.

I am positive that the operation was genuine. However, had

Kurt truly had such an infection or abscess, he would have been extremely ill.

Osolsobie had not told Mercado or any of his aides about the operation by Tony. Actually Kurt is certain that he was not truly opened by Tony. But how did Mercado know about the surgery? Why did Mercado discredit Tony, who is said to be his lifelong friend?

A later interview with Lolet, Mercado's chapel president and a "minor medium" who demonstrates phenomenon by lifting a large table with the flat of her hands, cast a little light on the matter. She said that Mercado, like Tony, was beginning to stick his hand out for donations from Americans. "The money goes into his pocket, not the church," she said with disdain. She said that Tony and Mercado were friends, but they often pretended bad blood to help Mercado pick up donations.

Both healers are from the same tiny village of Rosales. Mercado told me that Tony's version of becoming a healer was fiction. Mercado said: "I am ten years older than Tony. I taught him to heal." However, José Garcia, an elderly man from Rosales, said:

"Mercado is older than Tony and learned how to heal before Tony, but both of them are guilty of spreading a little fiction."

The clamor over Kurt's "infection" had hardly died down when a loud, unified gasp from the throng of natives in the chapel signaled something else extraordinary.

A Filipino woman about twenty years old was being escorted to the table. The diagnosis that created the stir was "witchcraft." We had heard of these fantastic materializations and had seen one in Don Wild's film of Tony and Marcello, but this was our first chance to observe the phenomenon.

Again Mercado worked rapidly on the patient's lower abdomen. The girl was not in pain, but she was evidently upset at the thought of being a witchcraft victim. She covered her face with her arm and sobbed convulsively during the operation. I leaned in for a closer look; my nose was about eighteen inches from the action. Suddenly several large, flat leaves from some tropical plant popped up from the surgical opening like a jack-in-the-box. I stared in blank disbelief as the crowd behind me gasped in unison. Mercado plucked the leaves out of the girl and waved them to the onlookers.

"Witchcraft," he explained with a toothy grin.

Kurt Osolsobie's eyebrows were raised—he too was seeing but not understanding. Jack Netchin, standing at the head of the table taking pictures, just shrugged and kept on filming. I picked up a leaf that had missed the wastebasket and examined it closely. It looked and felt like the leaf of a plant. It was spattered with blood and about ten inches long and three inches wide at its widest point. If Mercado had palmed the leaves, they would have been crumpled; that leaf was perfectly smooth. I'd already made routine checks of the sheet and the cotton. Before the girl got off the table, I examined her, with Lolet's help; the waistband of her skirt was tight. Those leaves *had* been inside the girl!

In Don Wild's film, Marcello Jainar removes about two feet of "plastic wrap" from a patient's abdomen as Tony looks on. The slowest of slow motion cannot detect any sleight of hand. Certainly it's illogical, but the whole phenomenon is illogical.

Brother Juanito Flores, another lowlands healer, also performed a witchcraft operation. We missed it, but Mac McEwen and Marla Kelly visited Flores in lieu of Marlyn and me, since we left the Philippines a few days early in order to visit Dr. Hiroshi Motoyama in Tokyo. I'm not at all sorry I visited Dr. Motoyama, but I wish I had seen Flores—his operations were spectacular. But since all three witnesses were somewhat skeptical at the time, I consider them fully objective.

"This guy was something else," McEwen reported. "He went into a trance, and it seemed to take a lot out of him, but when he worked, he showed us something."

The witchcraft operation that Flores performed was on a Filipino man's lower abdomen. McEwen said: "I saw it, but I don't go for it, Tom. I don't buy it; I didn't see any hanky panky, but I don't buy it."

Marla Kelly also refused to "buy" the phenomenon, but when her own epileptic condition improved considerably after surgery by Tony and treatment by Flores, she reconsidered. She describes the witchcraft operation:

"Flores opened the Filipino man's stomach and it looked like just another psychic surgery—funny how we can become so blasé about it after two weeks—until he started bringing out money. He picked up an old tablespoon and dug coins out of the man's body. It was as if he were scooping ice cream. When he was almost finished, he rammed the spoon clear down inside the man—it must have reached his backbone—and dug out one more coin."

I was told by one person that "those witchcraft operations ruin the credibility of the whole thing." In defense of these witchcraft claims I offer the following comment from a newspaper, taken from the wires of Associated Press and United Press International in 1972:

A team of North Vietnamese surgeons discovered a hideous creature living and growing inside the abdomen of a twenty-two-year-old man.

Dr. Ton That Tung and his associates removed the creature and put it to sleep. The monster weighed more than three pounds and was about ten inches in length, the North Vietnamese news agencies revealed.

It looked somewhat like a malformed iguana lizard. It had a large tongue capping its head and one big eye. Its jaws were poorly formed, but its teeth were well developed and sharp. It had two limbs, which resembled chicken legs.

The thing was located between the man's liver, his right kidney, and his right lung. Its neck passed through the man's diaphragm muscle, the news agency reported.

According to the news agency, Dr. Tung is experienced in monster removal. He performed a similar operation fifteen years ago.

Of course, there is the possibility of a hoax here. Many news stories are printed without verification, and news reporters with a warped sense of responsibility are common. On the other hand, many strange occurrences have been encountered by surgeons and left unexplained.

Mac and Marla described the conditions in Flores's chapel as "filthy and crawling with bugs."

On Saturday, June 25, 1972, they observed the services of Brother Juanito Flores, twenty-five years old, a member of the Espiritistas Union. They told of "spiritual injections" matching those we saw at Mercado's. Flores took his "needle" out of an open Bible.

When he diagnoses, Flores has an aide hold up the Bible while he wraps the patient in a white sheet and strides around gazing with his "third eye." He is in a trance when he works.

His chief assistant is Victoria Pozon, twenty years old, Lolet's daughter and a nursing student. She speaks excellent English. Her experiences with Flores have been amazing. She said:

"Juanito can bring down goblets from heaven [materializations], and I have seen the human heart pumping beneath his hands. I cannot say how it happens."

McEwen described how the spiritual vaccinations caused patients to wince, flinch, or jump. "He gave me a shot, and it hurt."

Victoria said that the injections need not be painful, but the healers like to give foreigners and doubters a jolt.

Like the other Espiritistas, Flores has special days for his services. He works only on Wednesday and Saturday mornings. There are times when he listens to his spirit guide and refuses to operate on any foreigners. He refuses donations for his healing because he makes a satisfactory living from carabao trading.

"I am only dealer with x ray eyes," he told McEwen with a grin.

McEwen, who took copious notes for me, noticed that Flores went through two stages when he healed. "First, he's light and has a pleasant bedside manner. He laughs and jokes with the patients and said he believes in a happy God. Second, when he's ready to operate, he's intense and working very hard."

The first major patient of the morning was Guido Pavan, a visitor from Venice, Italy. He had undergone orthodox surgery for spinal arthritis in January, 1971. He had high blood pressure and suffered a great deal of pain. Flores gave him four spiritual injections, which drew blood that stained his shirt and pants.

Flores diagnosed appendicitis: "You have a pain," he said pointing to Guido's torso. Guido agreed.

McEwen describes the operation:

"Guido was lying on his back. Flores didn't fool around with any cotton or other gimmicks; he used two fingers on each hand to gouge an opening in Guido's body. I watched from two feet away as he looped some intestine out of the hole with his left hand and worked on it with his right. He removed some gray matter from the intestine, and it stunk. I've seen guts before, and believe me, this was genuine. Flores had his assistant wipe his hands off while he left the intestine hanging out. Guido was wide awake. Flores emptied the insides of the intestine, and all his work was in plain sight. After he slid everything back into Guido's body, he worked inside briefly. Then he removed his hands, and the opening closed instantly. Guido said he felt a little pain, but it was not bad. Flores was tuckered out and went outside to rest and say some prayers."

Marla and McEwen watched also when Flores removed a foot-long tapeworm from a Filipino man's intestine. "We could see the intestines clearly from ten feet away. There was no doubt about Flores's openings," Marla reported.

A Filipino woman had an infected tooth socket, so Flores used a pair of small scissors to clean it out. These were the same scissors he had used moments earlier to clean his fingernails.

McEwen describes his own experience: "Flores didn't have the vocabulary to identify my atrophied spine, but he knew other healers had taken a crack at me, and he pointed out where they'd worked. He said he could see the cuts their work left. He didn't operate on me, saying that massage was enough because of the treatment by the other healers. He gave me a shot from that crazy Bible, and it really jolted me."

All three viewers agreed that Flores seemed to work more deliberately and slowly than Tony. He also removed a greater variety of materials than they had observed at Tony's; all three witnessed more operations by Agpaoa than I did.

There was a pause in the action while Flores recuperated. Marla was getting queasy—the filthy conditions, the gory operations, everything was upsetting. She no sooner had made her mind up to have nothing else to do with psychic surgery, headaches or no headaches, than she was told that she would be the next patient. McEwen watched from about ten feet away.

Flores had not asked nor had been told about Marla's headaches, but he diagnosed them and said they were caused by "sleeping with wet hair."

When he operated, he made two small incisions with his forefinger in the back of her neck. Then he lifted out and looped about a foot and a half of white fiberlike nerve tissue.

"He held the loop of tissue away from her body with one hand and swabbed it with cotton until the bloody bits, about the size of peas, were cleaned off. Then he eased it back into her body, as if it were on a spring, like a tape measure," McEwen said.

Marla said it had hurt when he made the incision and the opening felt hot while he worked. The operation left a mark; two white welts in a small oval field of red remained on Marla's neck for a few days. Then they vanished.

"I was scared to death," Marla admitted, "the place was filthy and crawling with flies and lizards; and Flores is more voodoo-like than Tony."

Equally as remarkable as the surgery he performed on her was Flores's ability to see inside and diagnose Marla's conditions. "After he looked me over, he pointed his finger at me and with no qualms demanded to know which healer had worked on me. I said Tony, and he said no, not that operation —the operation on my stomach. He said he could see the scars inside."

Marla has no scars on her abdomen, and she had forgotten about a 1965 cytosectomy that was performed when she had a kidney infection. Flores told her she couldn't fool him because he could see inside. Then she remembered. "There's no way he could have known about that except by really seeing inside of me."

Finally Flores prescribed a strict diet for Marla and told her not to bathe for five days. The orders were hard to follow, but today, after years of pain, Marla remains free of headaches.

One other supposedly incurable ailment was mysteriously cleared up. Marla had had a raw place on her right shin for nearly ten years, which physicians diagnosed as psoriasis in one instance and a leg ulcer in another. "Whatever it was, it oozed junk constantly and itched terribly." Though neither Tony nor Flores worked on it, by the final Saturday of the trip it was healed.

"The only one to touch it was old Moises, who rubbed it with that oil before he started propositioning me."

There is a brown oil and a white oil used by the Filipino healers. Both oils are multipurpose patent medicines manufactured in the Orient. The brown oil is "yee tin" and is manufactured in Thailand. The white oil is "pak fah yeow" and is manufactured in Singapore. Both oils are distributed throughout the Orient by a Hong Kong wholesaler. The white oil's ingredients are simple. The label reads: "menthol crystal, 10%; wintergreen oil, 40%; eucalyptus oil, 38%; camphor, 6%; and lavender oil, 6%."

The brown oil's ingredients are more complex. This is how they are listed by the manufacturer: "Food colouring, 3%; inula, 5%; boswellin carot, 4%; commiphora myrrna, 3.5%; clycyrrhiza, 5%; carthamusinetorious, 4%; lithospernum offi-cinale, 4.5%; leaf of artemisia, 5%; oil of artemisia, 5.5%; oil of tea seed, 10.5%; and oil of peppermint, 50%."

A tiny bottle of these oils costs about a quarter in Baguio City. The bottles last a long time because one shakes droplets out of small openings. The manufacturers claim that these oils effectively treat just about every ailment, internal and external. I've used it for internal problems such as nausea and flu symptoms. Two or three drops in a shot glass of water worked better than any American products I've tried. However, I'm seldom ill or upset, so my testimony doesn't apply to a wide range of ailments.

In Baguio Marlyn and I both happily discovered that the oils, when combined with a mild balm the healers also use, relieve sunburn pain. At first the applications create even more heat, but within minutes the oil begins to soothe the skin. The brown oil has also been effective in earache cases, and it's an excellent liniment, especially when mixed with the balm.

Perhaps it was this oil that helped Marla. Or maybe it was the acupuncture-style balancing that did it. There are reports from the Orient that acupuncture is effective against psoriasis.

Before leaving Baguio, McEwen and Kurt Osolsobie investigated the healing team of Robert Stent and Eddie Simbel, diagnostic specialists and "absent" healers. Stent, an Australian, has forsaken his Western life style to become a healer in Baguio. Simbel is a Filipino whose leg was saved from gangrene in World War II by a healer. He was so impressed by her powers that he devoted his life to healing. Simbel taught Stent what he knew, and Stent has incorporated other phenomena into their practice.

They guarantee accurate diagnosis and availability of a cure. They refuse donations and fear commercialism; they prefer making a living from renting rooms in their boarding house. They accept money when working absent healing by mail, but the stipend is used to defray postal expense.

"They were both honest and logical," reported Herb Johnston, who took his father-in-law, Alexander Klahre, to see them in hopes of determining the availability of his cure.

They use what Stent calls a "diagnoser," which he claims to have brought to Baguio from a temple in India. Whatever its background, the levitation displayed by this stone and mirror impressed and amazed the imperturbable Kurt Osolsobie.

Kurt writes: "Stent and Simbel are very sincere people. I cannot imagine that they don't really believe what they say. That moving stone on the mirror is spectacular psychokinesis. I examined the stone, the mirror, and the table before, during, and after the showing. No tricks!"

McEwen describes the mirror as an eight- by eleven-inch plate, and the pointer resembles an arrowhead. It's greenish-gray in color, with dark and light stripes. The stone glides across the face of the flat mirror without any apparent physical force.

"They dribble some water at the far end of the mirror; then they place the arrow in the water. You then put your fingers on the corners nearest you, about a half-inch from the edge," reported Mac. "When I tried it, Simbel held my wrist and tried to get the pointer to move closer to my fingers, but four inches from the starting point is all I could get out of it. I think this means I'll never totally recover."

The stone arrow zipped all the way across the mirror for Alexander Klahre and young Mike Jablonski, who are now accepting absent prayer healing from Stent and Simbel. Herb Johnston, skeptical at seeing the arrow move on the mirror, tilted the mirror. A steep angle was required to make it slide by gravity.

Miracle surgery, psychic diagnosis, faking and chicanery, materializations, levitations, and philosophical inconsistency—we had it all in Baguio. What's going on? Is there an explanation?

If any man can convince me and bring home to me that I do not think or act aright, gladly will I change; for I search after truth, by which no man ever was harmed. But he is harmed who abideth on still in his deception and ignorance. . . .

Marcus Aurelius

5 An Explanation

IT'S EASY to understand how so many people can build themselves a psychological wall in order to avoid any reasonable consideration of the subject of psychic surgery. It's also easy to see how a mythology grew up around psychic surgery and how many people believe all sorts of wonderful, perhaps partially true tales about healers.

And it is especially easy to understand how so many people jumped at conclusions and rapidly became convinced that the entire phenomenon is a hoax. All these psychological manifestations are comprehensible but difficult to deal with. Therefore, before diving into an explanation of what psychic surgery is, let's first consider everything it is not.

First, and probably most important, psychic surgery is *not impossible*. Our everyday framework of understanding misconstrues many facets of existence. Humans have a damnable ability to set up a thinking process that excludes large hunks of reality from the perception of the thinker. In this respect many phenomena generally assumed to be impossible are quite possible, but they are victims of the narrowest of premises.

The fascinating science of molecular biology has shown that the parting and rejoining of human body molecules shouldn't be impossible. There is research underway today into the idea of laser beam or electromagnetic surgery, which would not leave scar tissue. Biochemists and other researchers are finding that "thought" can affect the spirals of DNA, which are believed to hold the key to life.

Our present understanding of physics, which is constantly changing, and our use of atomic energy should be enough to force the notion of impossibility down the drain.

Second, psychic surgery is *not fakery*. The incidents in which faking has been proved beyond the shadow of a doubt are few and far between. Fakery has been alleged many times but proved only rarely. Claims of fakery are as subject to skepticism as are claims of genuine operations. Joe Pyne's claims, for example, are hysterical and unproved allegations.

Skepticism can be overdone. The natives in the heartland of Morocco, living in a primitive desert tribal culture, consider the Apollo moon landings to be a hoax. Even those who saw the events on television consider the Apollo flights to be nothing more than "Hollywood fakes." Those desert people are as positive that they are right as you and I are that the landings truly did happen.

When it comes to psychic surgery, the majority of Americans behave like the Bedouins of Morocco. Their narrow comprehension cannot assimilate the information; therefore, it must be a hoax.

Professional magicians have watched Agpaoa and other healers work for hours without detecting any sleight-of-hand artistry. Yet rank amateurs have claimed to catch the healers in the act of palming some bloody tissue. Of all the fakery claims, I accept only one as true—the testimony of Jack Netchin.

When we observed, we were fully aware of fakery charges, but we are as positive as it is possible to be without concrete clinical proof that no such chicanery took place in our presence. It is inconceivable that Tony would fake an operation so badly that it was readily detected by one man at a private demonstration yet still be so professional he could fool nearly everyone all the time. The inconsistency of the healing and the healers does create suspicion, but this inconsistency has another cause. Since the success of a healer is hard to explain, it stands to reason that the failures will be likewise hard to explain.

In a way Dr. Kurt Osolsobie is reacting much like the Moroccans, but his skepticism may be due to his extensive scientific training. Because of the nature of the lifelong training and work, the professional has a more difficult time assimilating all the ramifications of psychic surgery than does a nonprofessional. A person conditioned by "scientific technique" has difficulty accepting the unscientific conditions of psychic surgery.

Scientific technique has its place, but it is not infallible. Simon Newcomb, astronomer and mathematician of consummate ability, demonstrated "conclusively" that vehicles heavier than air could not fly. Two bicycle repairmen at Kitty Hawk proved Newcomb and theoretical mathematics to be wrong. It was the venerable Roger Bacon who said, "We can do much more than we know."

Dr. Osolsobie and Professor Hans Bender, of Germany, who also visited Tony Agpaoa, "assume" that Tony uses a specially prepared plastic foil when exhibiting what appears to be an open abdomen. No evidence of such a foil has been uncovered, but without any concrete proof Kurt to some degree and Bender quite adamantly feel that Placido, Mercado, Marcello, Terte, and Agpaoa all use sleight-of-hand work. In a letter to me Kurt wrote: "Flores, however, merits a question mark." Like the others who witnessed Juanito Flores, Dr. Osolsobie was impressed. "It was something other than sleight of hand," he said.

Kurt wrote also: "You asked me whether I really had gallstones. Yes, I had them; the x ray proved it. Perhaps I do not have them any longer—I do not know—but I will soon know. The troubles [symptoms] are improved since the treatment by Flores; but this can be subjective and have a passing-by effect."

Perhaps gallstones are not scientifically sound for testing purposes. The organic stones that infect gall bladders of thousands have proved confusing even to our orthodox physicians. For example, a woman in Sacramento, California, is suing four doctors for malpractice because they incorrectly diagnosed her condition as gallstones and operated. She didn't have gallstones; she was pregnant with her fifteenth child. It isn't surprising, then, to learn that she claimed the surgery for gallstones provided "no relief at all." There is no need to dwell on errors made by medical doctors; physicians are human and therefore subject to error.

Many detractors assume that psychic surgery is a hoax on the grounds that various laboratory analyses of tissue and blood removed by healers refuse to verify the phenomenon. In Manila every clinic you visit will tell you they have analyzed healers' specimens, and they're always "animal."

Such reports would be conclusive except for several obvious

inconsistencies. Careful diagnosis under controlled and objective conditions do not verify these clinical claims. In every account I've read that cited a laboratory analysis report calling the tissue or blood "animal," I could find no detailed documentation supporting the claim; and lab technicians fall prey to a little subjectivity, too.

With the help of a Filipino-American medical doctor who was in Baguio when we were, I carried out an informal placebo test on a clinic. Two genuine gallstones removed from a living patient were sent to a laboratory, but the clinic was informed that the stones had been removed by psychic surgery. The report came back without detailed analysis, but it carried a flat statement that the stones were not organic.

Despite modern technology and fantastic equipment, the laboratory examination techniques today are still primitive, according to many eminent researchers.

For example, a college student was serving as a research assistant to a highly respected and qualified doctor who was verifying a blood hypothesis. The student, working toward her degree in biochemistry, observed blood smears through one of the electron microscopes at the University of Illinois Medical Center, in Chicago. The student was particularly astute and sincere about reporting her observations. She discovered that her observations conflicted with the doctor's thesis. She discovered also that the first assistant, her supervisor, had been altering her reports so that her data confirmed the doctor's thesis.

One would think that the essence of science would triumph over such human frailty, that the doctor, when confronted with the evidence, would rebuke the first assistant and reward the dedicated technician. That wasn't the case. The student was declared incompetent without any semblance of a trial, and she was dismissed from her duties.

In the instance of psychic surgery the tissue or blood samples may indeed be "altered" and concluded to be "abnormal," but there is an explanation for this, which will be discussed later. The tissue is certainly not "animal," and the case for fakery is without merit.

Third, psychic surgery is *not hypnosis*. Earlier I commented that I was in no way hypnotized. There was a need to make such an observation; many learned people have the absurd notion that every patient of psychic surgery has been influenced by hypnotic suggestion. Of course, there are those who say that because we are all hypnotized, we know nothing of reality. Such a notion is a play on semantics and nothing else.

Hypnosis is like electricity, light, and other energy phenomena. We can use it; we can see manifestations that prove that it exists, but we don't know exactly what it is. The states of hypnosis are all we have to work with, and here the nomenclature is confused. Lethargic, somnambulistic, and cataleptic are the designations, but the order in depth of trance is often switched. Some say somnambulistic is the deepest state, and others say that cataleptic is deepest.

Many visitors to the Philippines have noted that Tony's room seemed "different." Others noted that the healer's aides rub oil and balm near the eyes in order to create a distraction. The rituals of the Espiritistas and the patients' own expectations all contribute to conditions ripe for "hypersuggestibility" on the part of the patients, they say. Persons who believe are ready to see miracles; those who scorn are ready to see fakery. This notion is perhaps acceptable, but can a camera lens be made hypersuggestive?

While photographs do not represent irrefutable evidence, cameras are excellent devices for exploring phenomena. If something is physical and reflects light, the lens catches it and imprints the film. One cannot hypnotize a camera lens. Photography has been an invaluable aid to many areas of research, including research into psychic surgery, and later we will see how a form of photography called "Kirlian" helps to verify the fact of healing energy.

If it were not for photographic evidence, hypnosis would be a very real solution possibility to the mystery of psychic surgery. The phenomenon of telepathic hypnosis, where the control is obtained without any apparent physical contact, has played a role in one of the world's most notorious phenomena—

the Hindu fakir's rope trick; and it was the camera's objective eye that supplied the proof.

Mordecai M. Merker, a New York attorney, suggests in an article that the famed rope trick and motion pictures combine to offer concrete proof of telepathic hypnosis. In reverse, motion pictures of psychic surgery prove that something physical does exist and that hypnosis is not a factor.

The November-December, 1971, issue of *Parapsychology Review* printed Merker's article. The lawyer cites studies by Dr. Alexander Pilcz, professor of psychiatry at the University of Vienna during the early 1900s; Dr. Rudolf von Urban, author of *Beyond Human Knowledge;* and Dr. Andrija Puharich, eminent researcher and the world's leading authority on the late José Arigo, a psychic surgeon in Brazil.

Dr. Pilcz, who was highly skeptical of telepathy, witnessed the rope trick performed by a fakir and a small boy. A rope was tossed into the air and appeared to suspend vertically and rigidly without support. The boy climbed the rope; then he dropped back to earth. The rope appeared to change into a pole, fall to earth, and break into many pieces. Finally the pieces appeared to reassemble, and the original rope reappeared. A miracle?

Not really. As Dr. Pilcz observed all these happenings in the company of others who saw the same thing, he was also taking motion pictures. Not a single scene he had observed appeared on the processed film. The fakir tossed the rope into the air, but it fell directly back to earth. The boy and the fakir remained motionless as the faces of the onlookers registered amazement at what they were seeing.

Dr. von Urban wrote of Dr. Pilcz's experience and concluded: "It appears, therefore, that the trick depends entirely on mass suggestion."

Being dedicated scientists, Dr. Pilcz and Dr. von Urban returned to India to investigate further. Their experiences are told by Dr. Puharich in his book *Beyond Telepathy:*

"All of the observers, including the scientists, saw the fakir throw a coil of rope into the air and saw a small boy climb up the rope and disappear. Subsequently, dismembered parts of this small boy came tumbling down to the ground; the fakir gathered them up in the basket, ascended the rope, and both the boy and the fakir came down smiling. It is astonishing that several hundred people witnessed this demonstration and agreed in general on the details as described. There was not a single person in the crowd who could deny these facts. However, when the motion pictures of this scene were developed subsequently, it was found that the fakir had walked into the center of the group of people and thrown the rope into the air, but that it had fallen to the ground. The fakir and his boy assistant had stood motionless by the rope throughout the rest of the demonstration. The rope did not stay in the air, the boy did not ascend the rope. In other words, everyone present had witnessed the same hallucination. Presumably the hallucination originated with the fakir as the agent or sender. At no time in the course of the demonstration did the fakir tell the audience what they were going to see. The entire demonstration was carried out in silence."

Merker also cites another scientist, Dr. Alexander Cannon, a physician who lived in the Orient and studied yoga. Dr. Cannon confirmed the Viennese scholars' experiences, writing in his book *Powers That Be,* in 1935:

"The trick does not take place. What happens is that a fakir impresses the mark of his own vivid imagination so strongly upon the surrounding sea of mental ether that every person who enters that sphere of influence is at once affected by it."

Merker believed that motion pictures and the ancient rope trick provided a solid case for telepathic hypnosis; conversely, motion pictures make a solid case against hypnosis in psychic surgery.

Still another scornful allegation made by doubters of psychic surgery is that motion picture films showing the operations are tampered with to look real. This is absurd. The number of home movies of psychic surgery in existence is impressive. It's absurd to believe that persons with no motive other than a conviction about a healing would go to considerable expense to have a film doctored for the purposes of perpetrating a hoax diametrically opposed to their beliefs.

Psychic surgery is not impossible, not fakery, not hypnotic suggestion, not a hoax. It is also *not a miracle*. The number of practitioners who have learned psychic surgery takes it out of the realm of miracles. A miracle implies something over and above natural law. It is our lack of understanding that makes some things seem miraculous.

The practice of psychic surgery is *not limited to the Philippines*. Arigo, who lived and practiced in Brazil, was every bit as knowledgeable and astonishing as any of the Filipinos. Various forms of the same kind of spiritual healing have been utilized by primitive shamans and witch doctors throughout the world. African witch doctors, Eskimo shamans, and Caribbean voodoo priests did not earn their reputations on the strength of public relations alone. Behind every legend is a spark of truth.

Even in our technically superb Western culture spiritual healers abound, people who astonish, confuse, and anger medical orthodoxy. England's Harry Edwards, for example, is hailed by his followers as the most prolific healer in the world. His enthusiastic following credits him with more than 13,000 documented cures.

Edwards and other British healers who boast that they are mediums have been engaged in a running battle with orthodoxy, and they finally gained the right to visit patients in hospitals if the patients requested it. Mediumship and healing in England are so popular that there is a weekly newspaper, called *Psychic News,* devoted entirely to the subject. On occasion the enthusiasm of the following leads to some unsubstantiated claims to be made in print. Biased reporting, like skepticism, can be a two-way street, but one shouldn't discard an entire field of study on the basis of over-enthusism on the part of a believer. It would be like disregarding all literature concerning natural food nutrition simply because one health food chain magazine cites how birds and wild animals "eat all the natural foods they want, but you never see an obese wild creature."

In France there is the renowned shrine at Lourdes which has drawn millions of infirm people from all over creation. It is said that the percentage of cures proportional to the number of visitors is unimpressive, and the biggest businesses are gift shops and funeral parlors. However, the relatively few dramatic healings that have occurred over the years make Lourdes synonymous with faith healing.

In Italy famed Fra Pio performed a healing ministry while demonstrating the phenomenon known as "stigmata," or unexplained bleeding from the palms of the hands, another widespread mystery akin to psychic surgery.

In the United States a number of well-documented healers perform regularly before massive audiences. The list includes Kathryn Kuhlman, Oral Roberts, Willard Fuller, Olga Worrall, and her late husband, Ambrose Worrall. There are literally hundreds of lesser known healers practicing in the United States. The healing phenomenon is not limited to the Philippines; it's as widespread as humanity.

So much for what psychic surgery is not. What is it?

We left the Philippines a few days ahead of our tour group, just ahead of the worst tropical storm in that nation's history, in order to spend a day with Dr. Hiroshi Motoyama at his Institute of Religious Psychology, in Tokyo. Dr. Motoyama is a psychologist, parapsychologist, theologian, and highly qualified practitioner of acupuncture. He has lectured and taught in the United States at Duke University and in India at Andhra University as well as in his native land. In May, 1970, he published a book on his seven years of researching Filipino psychic surgery, titled *Trips for Investigating Psychic Operations in the Philippines*. Accompanied by Jack Netchin, we toured Dr. Motoyama's institute and discussed his views on psychic surgery.

Under controlled conditions Dr. Motoyama patiently built an airtight case for the actuality of psychic surgery. His methods are up to date and precise, and his records are open to the world of science for verification.

Dr. Motoyama documented a psychic operation performed

by Juan Blanche. The documentation includes detailed laboratory analysis of tissue and blood samples and firsthand observation by qualified physicians in a medical clinic.

At Far Eastern University in Manila Juan Blanche performed psychic surgeries on three patients under controlled conditions while Dr. Motoyama, Dr. Enrique Ramos, and Dr. David M. DeLeon (pathologist) looked on. Blanche, whose spectacular method of opening is achieved by waving his forefinger or the forefinger of another person in the air above the part of the patient's body in which the incision is needed, operated on two epidermal cysts and a young girl's eye. Using only his fingers, Blanche removed a cyst from the back of Ramon Majno's neck in a short time. The cyst was immediately taken to the laboratory and analyzed. The same operation on a different patient followed, and the same procedures were repeated. The cysts were preserved and carried to the Tokyo University of Medicine for a second analysis.

The Far Eastern University hospital laboratory report, submitted by Dr. David DeLeon, dated September 28, 1968, reads as follows:

Specimen: Tissue from a lesion at the right int. scapula region.

Gross description: Multiple irregular fragments of brownish fibrofatty tissue with an aggregate volume of 3 cc. Representative portions are taken for embedding.

Microscopic description: Sections reveal normal fatty tissue without any enclosing capsule. In places are small strands of fibrous tissue. No significant inflammatory cell reaction is seen and no neoplastic characteristic is noted.

Histo Diagnosis: Normal fatty tissue.

Remark: This is either a normal subcutaneous fatty tissue or fragments of a benign lipoma.

Blood: Type A–Rbc show beginning hemolysis. Few leucocytes.

The laboratory report from Tokyo University included drawings of the sections and a detailed description. The histopathological diagnosis was "epidermal fatty cyst."

After operating on the girl's eye Blanche used a small water glass and a coin to help balance her body. He placed the glass on the middle of her back between the shoulder blades. An expert acupuncturist, Dr. Motoyama noted with keen interest what Blanche was doing. He commented:

"He accomplished a depletion at a viscero-cutaneous reflex point, which is a kind of treatment often done in acupuncture." Depletions in the flow of yin and yang are often necessary to effect a balance in the patient's subtle system.

Back in Baguio, McEwen had watched Placido use a water glass and "fire" to treat a patient. McEwen concluded that it was nothing more than a sideshow trick using a vacuum principle. Placido dropped some alcohol or lighter fluid on the patient's abdomen and struck a match to it (it doesn't burn unless the patient gets panicky and starts jumping around). In a few seconds he snuffed the flames out with the water glass, thus creating a vacuum, which in turn sucked some fat part up inside the glass, giving the appearance of levitation. It's hard to tell if it was a trick or a depletion. Dr. Motoyama pointed out that Blanche didn't use any fire, yet some skin and flesh did appear to be pulled up into the glass.

Laboratory analysis of blood samples obtained from a patient of the late psychic surgeon Ricardo Gonzales brought positive results, too. Dr. Motoyama said, "Blood samples obtained before and during the operation were compared and proved to be the same."

However, the results of comparative blood samples from an American patient operated on by Tony could not be identified with each other. Dr. Motoyama reasoned that Tony's use of alcohol and water during the operation may have altered the blood sample slightly.

While in Tokyo, Dr. Motoyama told us he had inserted his finger into psychic incisions "more than three centimeters" deep while Tony was performing. In summarizing all his evidences, Dr. Motoyama said: "I infer that the psychic operations have been true."

Electronic devices also provide ample proof that psychic surgery is effective. A nine-year-old epileptic named Jeffrey,

before psychic operation
(in Chicago)

SUPERIOR TEMPORAL

ANTERIOR TEMPORAL

**EEG before
psychic operation.**

LP Jeffrey 1 week after psychic operation (at The Institute of Religious Psychology)

RP

LT

RT

**EEG one week after
psychic operation.**

Jeffrey T. 2 weeks after psychic operation
(in Chicago)

**EEG two weeks after
psychic operation.**

Tomaszek.

who was operated on by Gonzales under Dr. Motoyama's surveillance, was monitored by an electroencephalograph (EEG) in Chicago prior to the operation. An EEG reading was made in Tokyo one week after the surgery, and considerable improvement was indicated. Two weeks after the operation another EEG reading was taken, this time back in Chicago. The latter reading showed additional improvement, especially in the "left temporalis, where apparent epileptic patterns had previously registered."

Two months after the psychic operations on his brain the boy was able to attend school full time. His previously expressionless face became expressive and animated.

Another patient, a man with a tumor in his spine, was x rayed prior to psychic surgery performed by Gonzales. The tumor showed up clearly. The patient had been unable to walk or move his arms well before the operation. After surgery the x rays showed that the tumor was gone, and the patient returned to work on his farm.

At his institute Dr. Motoyama showed Marlyn, Netchin, and me his laboratory, in which he tested Tony Agpaoa in 1966. Today the anteroom is a "Faraday cage," an enclosure that is lead-lined to prevent physical energies from passing through the walls. In the 1966 experiments Tony acted as a subject transmitting psychokinetic energy to other individuals, eight Japanese volunteers.

The participants were wired so that concurrent readings of galvanic skin response (GSR), EEG, plethysmogram, and pneumatograph could be constantly observed by the experimenter. The volunteers were unable to communicate by any sensory means without detection by the experimenters. Changes in the electronic monitors brought about by sensory stimuli were omitted from the data. Neither subject was informed of the nature or purpose of the experiment. Tony was told only that on a given electronic signal he was to transmit his healing power to the volunteer in the other room until a subsequent signal told him to relax.

After both subjects had been monitored in a quiet and re-laxed state for three minutes, Tony was given the high sign, and he transmitted for one minute. The experiment was re-peated many times over several days, and the results were significant, indicating that Tony Agpaoa indeed had some kind of ability to influence physiological functions of another person.

Here, in Dr. Motoyama's own words, is his explanation of the significance of the experiments:

"Taking GSR is to see the state and the working of the sympathetic nerve, which is one of the autonomic nerves. When the sympathetic nerve gets excited and strained, it causes the heart to palpitate. The respiration of the Japanese subjects became very fast suddenly from the moment when a signal was given to Tony to make mental concentration upon the subjects.

"Eventually the respiration of the percipient became con-fused; that is to say, sometimes it became slow and sometimes fast, and gradually the GSR showed a great change, which means that the sympathetic nerve was strained. From the mo-ment Tony stopped sending his mental power to the subject, the subject's respiration suddenly slowed, and the excitement of the sympathetic nerve decreased slowly."

Similar tests on yogis have been conducted in various Amer-ican labs, such as Dr. Elmer Green's facility at the Menninger Foundation, in Topeka, Kansas. These tests show that the hu-man mind in certain cases does indeed have an ability to in-fluence not only the yogi's physiology but the physiology of an individual who is concentrated upon. This fact can be a trifle frightening. Can we infer that witchcraft may indeed have hit upon this facet of mental control and indeed have created what is commonly called a *hex?* Furthermore, can it be inferred that this heretofore unsuspected power of mind might indeed be concentrated or magnified in order to separate the cells of a body and return them after a psychic operation?

Dr. Motoyama doesn't allow his enthusiasm to cloud his judgment. He takes his research seriously, and at this time he has linked psychic surgery with other known and tested phe-nomena—yoga and acupuncture.

"My hypothesis regarding the mechanism of psychic surgery is based upon the chakra [wheel] of yoga and the meridian of acupuncture," he explained.

Dr. Motoyama stresses that all the healers claim to have made a contact with a god or higher being through years of asceticism. (Tony claims to have fasted for extraordinary lengths of time.) It is this contact that gives them the ability to heal. Dr. Motoyama notes that yogis undergo years of asceticism in order to "awaken chakras" and accept "prana," a universal vital force through the aroused chakras. Prana converts to a physical energy and flows from the chakras through the "nadi," which are equivalent to meridians of acupuncture, into internal organs, peripheral tissues, and finally the brain. Consequently, Dr. Motoyama stated, advanced yogis can cure other individuals' illnesses by using prana.

Psychic healers evidently awaken chakras and accept prana, which in turn can be transmitted via the nadi, or acupuncture meridians, into the affected part of a patient's body.

This thesis would be little more than reasonable conjecture were it not for some experiments conducted by Dr. Motoyama that link yoga and acupuncture and define man's "vital," or second, body.

The various chakras said to exist in the "subtle" body of each individual must be verified. Yoga technique is demonstrably capable of controlling the autonomic nervous system, normally not consciously controllable. Advanced yogis have shown a remarkable ability to stop and restart their heartbeats and breathing over a prolonged period of time. The chakras are traditionally associated with the plexi of the physical body.

However, nadi, or acupuncture meridians, are not associated with the physical nervous system. They are part of a separate vital body energy system.

To prove the existence of acupuncture meridians and their detachment from the nervous system, a Japanese physician named Nagahama traced needle "echoes" throughout the body of a patient who was hypersensitive to the pain of needle in-

sertion. Dr. Motoyama, who has invented an electronic acupuncture "diagnoser" soon to be on the market, carried
Nagahama's tests a step further to prove that the meridians do
not coincide with the nervous system. Using electronic stimula-
tion and monitoring devices, Dr. Motoyama electrified a meridian called Sanshoboketsu simultaneously with the sympathetic
nerves distributed in the tip of the fourth finger. He summarized
his experiment as follows:

"It was revealed that a close reaction-relation exists between
Sanshoseiketsu, Sanshoyu, and Sanshoboketsu [all meridians]
but no close relationship to the system according to Western
neurology. According to Western medicine, there is no relationship between the tip of the fourth finger and the "dermatom of
L1 or the dermatom of T11."

Thousands of years of acupuncture experience has revealed
to Oriental practitioners that "ki," or prana, flows through more
than known physiological systems to keep the body alive. A
psychic healer can evidently control accepted prana and let it
flow into his patient's body through the meridians of acupuncture.

More recent studies by Soviet and American researchers
have utilized "Kirlian photography" to document further the
"vital body" idea. The Kirlian method of photography is to use
a strip of film, to place the object on the film, and to pulse
electrons through the object. In the Sunday, July 30, edition of
the *Los Angeles Times* Harry Nelson, the *Times* medical
writer, featured a detailed article of studies at UCLA's Neuro-
psychiatric Institute under the direction of Dr. Thelma Moss,
one of the world's leading parapsychologists.

The article stated that at UCLA scores of Kirlian photographs that show "coronas that seem to ebb and flow around
a faith healer's fingertips" have been taken. The author included
the following statement: "Psychic surgery—surgery without benefit of scalpel or anesthesia or trace of a scar—may not be fakery,
some serious minded people believe."

Using the same thesis, that a healer can transmit a force or
energy to an ill person, Dr. Moss and Dr. Marshall Barshay, a

kidney specialist on the staff of the Veteran's Administration, studied the reputed healing abilities of Yehuda Isk, an Israeli who bills himself as "the man with electric hands."

Remarkable photos, some displayed in the *Times,* documented the healer's effect on the leaf of a plant. Pictures showed also a loss of energy from the healer's fingers after a healing but an energy gain in the fingers of the patient.

Dr. Moss explained that nonhealers as well as the healer were tested. The photographic results showed that though everyone has a corona, the healer's corona was "quantitatively different."

In the Soviet Union this mysterious energy is called "bioplasma," and with the use of electronic devices Russian scientists have corroborated Dr. Motoyama's conclusions about the system of this vital force's being unrelated to the nervous system.

One of the major offshoots of research into yoga phenomena and relationships to the physiology has been *bio-feedback.* While many thousands of Americans are now part of the craze and are wiring themselves up to listen for a signal that will help them reach the alpha brain wave state and therefore learn to relax, many specialists are using the principle to accomplish over a period of time what some psychic surgeons have done in a matter of minutes.

At the University of Southern California, Dr. Alberto Marinacci has used bio-feedback techniques to reveal dormant muscle functions to persons who "believe" they are paralyzed. Dr. Maurice Sterman, of the huge Veteran's Administration center in Los Angeles, has been able to train severe epilepsy victims to prevent seizures by reconditioning their brain waves through bio-feedback response training.

Psychic surgeons have cured both epilepsy and paralysis; did they incorporate some of the principles being utilized by bio-feedback researchers today?

Other aspects of psychic surgery that may be explained by the "vital energy" concept are the lack of infection and the detection of certain unexplained changes in the blood of various patients.

Tony told our tour group that Dr. Hans Naegali, a parapsychologist from Zurich, Switzerland, who studied the Filipino healers at length, had presented a small flask of his blood to the healer and requested Tony "concentrate his power on it." The healer placed his hand over the flask, sent his concentrated energy into it, and, according to reports, caused changes in the specimen.

Such heretofore overlooked evidence could well account for any actual laboratory tests that showed differences in the blood and tissue samples from the same patient before and during psychic surgery.

Tony told us also that if he were to insert his hands into a sealed container filled with bacteria and virus specimen, the germs would be killed within moments. After seeing the unsanitary conditions under which the healers work, one certainly cannot doubt that their powers kill germs in some fashion.

An experiment conceived and conducted by Sister Justa Smith, a Franciscan nun who is chairman of the natural sciences department at Rosary Hill College, in Buffalo, New York, has shown that healers' hands indeed have an astonishing effect on body biochemistry.

Allen Spraggett, another journalist/psychic researcher, wrote of Sister Justa's experiments in the *Toronto Sun*. Her purpose was to determine if healers could affect enzyme activity—a precise functional activity in every body—with the energy from their hands and if so, in what way? Sister Justa has her doctorate in biochemistry with a specialty in enzymology; her experiments have been precise and probing.

Working with a Canadian healer named Oskar Estebany, she first experimented with trypsin enzymes, those controlling protein digestion. For seventy-five minutes each day over an eleven-day period Estebany held a sealed flask of trypsin. Result: he stimulated the activity of the enzymes dramatically. This discovery is significant because stimulated trypsin would increase the body's ability to digest protein and therefore would lead to a more healthful condition.

Like Dr. Moss, Sister Justa Smith experimented also with persons claiming no healing power. There was no change in the enzymes. Wanting to check the "intelligence" of the healing activity, she took her experiments two steps further. Some enzymes become overly active, and to effect a healing the activity should be retarded, not enhanced.

She used NAD, an enzyme that affects metabolism. A decrease in the activity of NAD would benefit the sick patient. True to the scientific method, Sister Justa did not inform the healers of the purpose of the experiment; she simply asked the three participating healers to pray over flasks of NAD. The same time span as in the initial experiment was observed. The result was remarkable: the healers had influenced the NAD in the proper direction; they had decreased its activity.

Finally, Sister Justa tested the clincher. She repeated the experiment with amylase-amylose, the enzymes responsible for controlling the amount of glucose released into the bloodstream. An increase in activity would lead to a diabetic condition; a decrease in activity, to low blood sugar. For optimum effect there should be no change. Sister Justa used the enzymes from the blood of the three healers, and when the experiment was completed, the result showed no change or effect on the enzymes—as it should be.

These tests would be equally effective if attempted with Filipino healers. Perhaps practitioners of orthodox medicine can eventually be persuaded to provide the means to test healing extensively. Allen Spraggett's comment at the end of his column suggests good reason for researching healers thoroughly:

"Sister Justa's experiments have far-reaching implications for medicine and all science. They suggest that healing hands are fact. Human thought can generate a force that heals. And this force is marvelously selective in its effects on specific bodily processes."

The "laying on of hands" healing technique seems to be explained by the experiments by Dr. Motoyama, Dr. Moss, Sister Justa, and the Russians, but they have not accounted for the opening and closing of the body and the tissue removal demonstrated in psychic surgery. To do so we must dip into an ancient idea, the concept of various levels of existence.

According to mystics, man has a number of bodies. This theory of co-existing levels of existence has been around as long as history. Christianity modified the concept over the years so that now the notion of planes of existence is classified under the subject of the occult and therefore off base for "normal" thinkers. In fact, however, the Christian concepts of body, spirit, and soul were sprawned by the planes-of-existence thesis.

The success of acupuncture anesthesia, the autonomic control attained by a yogi, mental influence on the spirals of DNA, telepathic hypnosis, and psychokinesis cannot be explained on the basis of the physical laws we presently understand. A reconsideration of the ancient concept of levels of existence must be undertaken.

Astronaut Edgar Mitchell has resigned from NASA to devote his life to research into human consciousness. He advocates the "systems" approach, as opposed to the compartmentalizing and isolating approach to phenomena-related study. Mitchell stated that physicists are already being forced to consider the planes-of-existence concept. He believes that scientists who assume that "all the basic physical laws have been discovered, and we need only apply them correctly to understand all nature," are incorrect. Mitchell's life was in the hands of these scientists when he rode to the moon and back on Apollo XIV, so his straightforward statements are startling to many. Mitchell's point is that despite our great understanding, we still run into unexplained phenomena and scientific dead ends when we deal with human consciousness.

With acupuncture, psychic surgery, and yoga as evidence, it may be inferred that information formerly considered "mystical" has merit. Before one considers this line of reasoning unacceptable, one must remember how "far out" Einstein's reasoning had to be to conclude his theories, which revamped our understanding of natural law.

While in the Philippines I asked Tony Agpaoa, David Oligani, and Joaquin Cunanan to explain the mechanics of psychic surgery as they understood them. Tony and Oligani are practitioners, but they differ extensively in method and character (Cunanan is the vice-president of the Espiritistas Union, and he has been a student of yoga, spiritualism, and healing for more than thirty years).

In essence the Filipinos explained that man is made up of many bodies; the "Holy Spirit," from a vantage point on high, works through the healers to operate and cure by effecting the necessary changes. Tony and the others accept the concept that our physical bodies fit a pattern, or matrix, formed on another level of existence. This second body is called by various names, including *vital body* and *etheric body*.

"If the vital body is opened by a spirit guide working through the healer [mediumship], the physical body will follow the pattern and open also. But this does not have to be so dramatic; many times vital surgery can take place without bleeding or incision. Our healers open the body primarily to dramatize the healing for the patient's benefit," Cunanan explained.

"Yes, I merely plant the seed. The mind of the patient really provides the cure," agreed Agpaoa.

Oligani, who has no education and only occasional contact with culture outside his village, said: "If the patient's higher self does not seek a cure, there will be no cure. Our angels know these things, and only God can cure."

Let's convert an ancient religious concept into a workable scientific hypothesis that fits rationally around all the areas of phenomena. Though seven planes, or levels, of existence coexist between God and man, man is involved with only the lower four—the physical, etheric, astral, and mental planes. An incarnate Ego (the created individual) is literally four bodies in one. The atoms of each level have a different nutational rate, which allows them to co-exist in the same apparent space. The rate of nutation increases in steps upward from the physical; there is no rapport obtainable by atoms of a slower rate with higher levels, but under certain conditions higher rates may seek a rapport with lower levels. Between the physical dwelling level for incarnate Egos and the astral dwelling place for decarnate Egos is the etheric, or vital, plane. The etheric level is not a dwelling level, but it is the home of gravity, which, though a weak force, profoundly affects the physical plane. Gravity is instantaneous and all-pervasive, inexplicable by the accepted notions of "pulling or pushing."

The one aspect setting man apart from the remainder of the physical plane, an obvious fact, is that man is created from the fourth level, in which he obtained the qualities of Mind. Since a higher plane can achieve a rapport with a lower plane, these qualities of mind allow man to experience events that appear to defy natural laws of time, space, and matter. These experiences are baffling to many people due to ignorance of the planes of existence. For example, telepathy has been demonstrated to be mind-to-mind communication. However, it cannot be measured or monitored with physical equipment consisting of atoms of the physical nutational rate, so in our physically oriented consciousness we are forced to doubt the evidence no matter how convincing it appears.

Psychic surgery, improbable according to physical laws alone, is acceptable and easily understood under the laws of the universe, which include natural laws for all the planes of existence. It would thus be worthwhile for all of science if mathematicians began to make experimental computations with the notion that there are several levels of existence.

Why contemplate four or more levels of existence when one more, the "body two," may be enough? My reasoning is that if mystics have been found accurate in respect to the vital body, it is wise to include other aspects of their thinking early in the game. If we are to use a systems approach to phenomena research, enough scope must be incorporated to cover all the bases.

The existence of a matrix on another level of existence accounts for the separating and rejoining of body tissue in psychic surgery; how, then, do we account for the "witchcraft" operations?

Dr. Hans Naegali, a Swiss psychiatrist, has a thesis. At Hot Springs, Arkansas, during the Memorial Day weekend in 1972, Dr. Naegali, Dr. Alfred Stelter of West Germany, and Dr. Motoyama attended Harold Sherman's annual conference on ESP and healing. At a private luncheon Dr. Naegali and Dr. Stelter gave a preview of their forthcoming research papers on psychic surgery.

"The materials removed are a materialization. The healer is a medium, and his guiding entity materializes the necessary parts to make the operation appear genuine. This is why some samples from operations often defy analysis," Dr. Naegali said. His thick German accent and highly enthusiastic manner gave him an appearance reminiscent of one of Hollywood's "mad scientists." Perhaps his theory is "mad" in the eyes of many, but it has substance. Naegali does not believe that materialization is the answer in every case, and Dr. Motoyama believes that not every surgery will prove to be "truly physical."

"We have a little of both, depending upon the spirit guide and the patient's needs," they agreed.

Dr. Naegali, a psychiatrist, is the head of the Zurich Parapsychological Society. During his visit to the Philippines he worked alongside Professor Bender, the best known European parapsychologist. Dr. Bender returned from his investigation to present a "one-sided and biased viewpoint that psychic surgery is nothing more than sleight-of-hand fakery," said Naegali and Stelter.

Dr. Bender's attack on the Filipino healers was reminiscent of the tactics of interviewer Joe Pyne; he accused them of fakery, but he offered no evidence to support his charge. Bender assumes that Tony used a specially prepared plastic foil. The professor's reasoning smacks of a man whose brain rejects information and frantically seeks to rationalize the rejection.

During his investigations Dr. Naegali encountered all the usual research-related problems. He said that he was quite confused when some blood samples of patients were reported by a Zurich laboratory to be "animal."

"I knew this could not be. I had witnessed the removal from the patient. I discovered that the albumin curves had been altered; to me this could have been due to radiation in the healer's hands, and it certainly did not justify the analysis as animal blood."

Dr. Naegali noted that psychic surgeons "penetrate the body without brutal force or instruments; in this respect it is similar to apport phenomena, in which a stone penetrates a wall or another stone." However, the key to Naegali's thesis came to him when he observed eggshells, coffee grounds, and even a crayfish being removed from a patient's body.

"*Bewitched* is what the Filipinos believe," he said, "but it is a materialization, a process by which thought forms are converted into something material."

In England, where seances are very popular these days, a materialization is considered the ultimate in mediumship. If Dr. Naegali's thesis is correct, the Filipino healers make the darkened room trance mediums look unimpressive indeed. Dr. Naegali's theory brought to mind the statement made by Victoria Pozon, assistant to Juanito Flores: "Brother Juanito can bring down silver goblets from heaven."

The materialization thesis needs more study. There is some circumstantial evidence, such as samples of tissue vanishing from containers, but there isn't enough to draw any substantial conclusion. The one thing to bear in mind is that materialization is *not* impossible. Noted yogi Indra Devi wears a string of pearls that were "precipitated from the ethers" by Sai Baba. The pearls have been amply analyzed; materialization is possible.

Scientific analysis answers some questions and explains some of the facets of psychic surgery, and the conjecture regarding planes of existence provides a consistent, workable hypothesis. Such a premise is sorely needed because up to now only mystics and "weirdos" have ventured into the realm of ultraconsciousness. Phenomena have been largely explained away by orthodoxy with subconscious or conscious premises.

Bergier and Pauwels write: "The spectrum of light is composed as follows: on the left, a wide band of Hertzian and infrared waves; in the center a narrow band of visible light; on the right, an infinite band ranging from ultra-violet, X and gamma rays to the unknown.

"And what if there were a comparable spectrum of intelligence, of human light? On the left, the infra, or subconscious; in the center, the narrow band of consciousness, and on the right the infinite band of the ultra-conscious. . . .

"One cannot explain the right hand portion of the light-spectrum in terms of the left hand portion—the gamma rays cannot be compared to Hertzian waves; their properties are not the same. Therefore, we think that if there is a state above and beyond that of our waking consciousness, the properties of the intelligence in that sphere will be totally different, and it will be necessary to devise other methods for their exploration than those employed in ordinary psychology."

While orthodox scientists must give themselves a little open-minded leeway in which to research phenomena, it is true that some inconsistencies regarding the healers and their practices cannot be explained by the scientific approach alone.

On the other hand, why should science shoulder the burden of our thinking? As physicist Dr. Stelter pointed out, "Everything outside physics has been treated as unscientific, and the scientific community seems to be reacting by growing more and more removed from man himself. Practically all we feel and experience is unacceptable by clinical standards."

It is not necessary to eliminate reality in order to prove what is real; therefore, to explore what psychic surgery is all about, we must understand the philosophy behind it.

No stream rises higher than its source. Whatever man might build can never express nor reflect more than he was. It was no more than what he felt. He can record neither more nor less than he has learned of life . . . his philosophy, true or false, is there.

Frank Lloyd Wright

6 The Search for Meaning

KATHRYN KUHLMAN, gospel minister and the epitome of American faith healers, raised her arm into the stream of light and from center stage front exhorted her audience to revel in the glory of God. Tears welled in her eyes as she mused in loud and pitying tones:

"Why do they have to analyze everything? Can't they see that it's God working here? Can't they see these wonderful miracles?"

To the mind of Kathryn Kuhlman, "they" include anyone who observes her healing ministry and ponders the reason of it all. A person who asks for explanations is disconcerting to her. To an evangelist it is almost heresy to wonder why "miracles" occur.

But we humans have been endowed with minds, and inherent in the mind are qualities that make blind, unreasoning faith difficult to obtain. A person needs to be thoroughly conditioned to achieve blind faith.

In the living room of Tony Agpaoa's home Rosita Rodriguez said to me: "Why should I have to act as an attorney for God? Why does God need any explaining or defense?"

Weary of fending off skeptics and detractors who constantly harass the healers, Rosita was stressing the fact that psychic surgery is "obviously" the work of God. Who are we, mere mortals, to challenge the mechanics of His work?

Everyone wants to know why. If God, in His omnipotence, decides to work astonishingly and obtrusively by "gifting" certain people with abilities to perform psychic surgery, why does he allow so many inconsistencies? There are those who believe that the devil put inconsistencies into the mechanics of God working through people in order to confound. There are others who believe that the same devil actually controls all phenomena in order to turn people away from the truth.

In our present pursuit of truth we have moved away from

the realm of science and are now diving headlong into the never-never land of belief and opinion, in which logic and reason only occasionally surface. However, with psychic surgery we are dealing with a phenomenon in which belief plays a key role. The term *faith healing* is not accidental.

Orthodox medicine recognizes the reality of psychosomatic illness—the unique ability humans have to create a physical ailment by thinking hard enough about it. It isn't usually direct thought; conscious activity triggers our subconscious mind, and our subconscious, without reasoning ability, goes to work on our vital body and causes physical malfunctions. Modern medicine does not explain it quite that way, but the concept of a vital body does add a degree of logic lacking in the standard thesis.

Orthodox scientists reason that those ailments created by our minds may be cured by somehow reversing the mental processes. Psychoanalysis was born when Sigmund Freud observed a patient overcome paralysis created by her subconscious. The existence of psychosomatic illness is no longer questioned, but its extent is often debated. For example, dermatologists disagree on the exact role played by the mind in allergy cases.

Long before medical science accepted the reality of psychosomatic causes, simple people knew that faith could cure illness and that the devil could cause it. It is commonly believed that those who have faith, those who believe without question that God is taking good care of them, can be cured through prayer or some related ritual form.

Tony Agpaoa insists that the mind of the patient determines the "complete" cure; he merely plants the seed with psychic surgery. If our mental processes, as yet not fully understood, can make us ill, they most certainly can make us well.

During my interview with Bill Monaghan, the AMA investigator, I mentioned Kathryn Kuhlman's heralded healings. Monaghan said: "She's been known to cure sickness or ailments of psychosomatic origin but nothing physical."

I don't really think he meant to imply that because something is psychosomatic, it is not physical.

What was revealed by my investigations of Kathryn Kuhlman refutes both the AMA claim that she heals only problems of psychosomatic origin and the common belief that the patient must have faith in a Christian God.

Kathryn Kuhlman does not divulge her age, but she must be well into her sixties. She's based in Pittsburgh, Pennsylvania, but she goes on the road much of the time, drawing huge crowds wherever she appears. In four appearances at the Arie Crown Theater in Chicago's McCormick Place the people who were turned away numbered in the thousands. There was no admission charge; the expenses were defrayed adequately by passing the hat.

I attended her late spring appearances with full intentions of documenting any healings I saw. However, I saw far too many to document without an army of reporters, so I selected five outstanding examples. If you've not attended a Kathryn Kuhlman revival complete with choir music, preaching, and healing, you've missed one of the most fantastic shows on earth.

The Arie Crown Theater holds about 5,000 people, and at each of her performances there was standing room only. It was even crowded backstage, with 200 or more choir volunteers and many special guests. Each side of the theater has an extensive area in which patients in wheelchairs may view the stage. Both sides were packed solid with patients of every sort—from seriously retarded children to wheezing geriatrics.

The expectations of the crowds make mood-setting easy. Before Kuhlman appears, the audience is put into a proper frame of mind with organ music and singing. Within a few seconds after her entry, Kathryn Kuhlman has nearly every individual in the audience held captive. She has a masterful stage presence; she uses drama to reach the people, and she knows what she's doing. Sometimes her voice is a whisper, barely audible even with the microphone; then she suddenly assails a point with a loud, pleading quality. Just as suddenly she exudes to a powerful, commanding presence.

"I am merely a woman—I do nothing. The things you witness here are the work of God," she drums into her audience over and over, at least once in each voice level. She wears a shimmering white dress with full-length billowing sleeves, which accentuate her timely and practiced gesticulation.

When the time for her healing is near, she warns her audience that she may stop in mid-sentence to announce that a healing has occurred. It's her way of preparing them for any spontaneous, uncontrolled healings. She usually begins the healing session by announcing that miracles have already taken place among the audience.

"A man somewhere in the balcony has a truss on. Take it off! You no longer need it. Where are you? Take off that truss and throw it away. There is a deaf person down here somewhere who can hear me. Yes, others who were deaf can now hear the sound of my voice. Those who were deaf but can now hear me, stand up! Where are you?"

On she goes, exhorting those who are suddenly healed to join her on the stage. She rambles through other spontaneous healings, ranging from arthritis of the big toe to extremely serious cancer cases. The crowd stirs slowly at first; then exclamations of "Oh, my God, I'm cured," may be heard throughout the throng. The ushers go to work, seeking out those who have truly remarkable cures and guiding them to center stage to meet Kathryn Kuhlman and be observed as "one of God's miracles."

On a given night as many as a hundred persons could conceivably go on stage to testify to a healing. I saw at least a hundred ushered to the stage and I selected five cases to document, all of whom testified that they received remarkable cures.

Julia Laurie, of Chicago, was escorted to center stage by an usher and her husband, Angelo Laurie. She was in a wheelchair, unable to walk because of lack of equilibrium. She had been a cancer patient for nine years, and her larynx had been removed in 1971. The cancer inside her head caused excruciating pain, which remained unchecked by drugs. The disease affected her equilibrium and caused deafness.

"She was sleeping in her chair," her husband explained, "and when Miss Kuhlman said that the deaf could hear, she woke up suddenly and told me she could hear."

Angelo Laurie had persuaded his wife to attend the healing in hopes of getting a miracle cure. He is a devout Catholic, and he had prayed for God's help. "I told my wife that if she could hear, we should go down to the stage and get everything fixed up." On the stage it appeared his prayers had been answered. Julia stepped from her wheelchair and walked gracefully as Kathryn Kuhlman encouraged her and told her she was an example of "God working among us." Julia Laurie could hear and walk, and she was relieved from the excruciating pain. Tears streamed down the sides of her face, and the audience cheered and praised God.

A week later I telephoned Julia Laurie's physician, who said: "I'm truly happy for her that the pain is gone. It's certainly in the realm of the miraculous; what more can I say? We considered a nerve block, but if we severed the nerve to kill the pain, she would be unable to swallow. She had most definitely lost her hearing due to the malignancy."

A month later I checked again. The pain had returned, but Julia Laurie could still hear and walk. Her husband said that he was "thinking of taking her to the Philippines, where there is a spiritual healer who can remove the tumor without damaging the rest of her." I did not comment.

Mitchell Teal, a seven-year-old boy from Muncie, Indiana, was the second case of the evening. Twice he had gone under a surgeon's scalpel to correct severely crossed eyes, the first time when he was only four and a half months and the second time at age four. He was scheduled for a third surgery in June, 1972, but it was not required.

When Mitchell walked onto the stage with his mother to announce that his eyes were miraculously straightened, I looked. They were indeed straight. "I was prepared for this to happen," cried Margaret Teal, his mother. "God instructed me to bring him here."

The physician who twice operated on Mitchell said that he examined the boy in March, a month before the healing session, and at that time he reluctantly recommended the third surgery. He had not examined the boy since the healing.

"If God has helped, I'm sure glad for the boy," the doctor said. "He had an awful deviation when I last saw him, and I wasn't certain that more surgery would correct the problem. I honestly believe the fusion centers for the eyes in the boy's brain are not well developed." Mrs. Teal canceled the surgery, and the doctor said: "God's help is appreciated. I need the time a lot more than the business."

It has been my experience that individual physicians are neither as dogmatic nor as adamant in their skepticism as are the officials of the AMA.

The case of Usha Tripathi, a Hindu woman who speaks no English, is the best example of evidence that Kathryn Kuhlman's healing sessions are not totally a matter of belief or hysteria. Usha and her sister-in-law attended the session merely to observe. Usha Tripathi is not a Christian, and since the English language was foreign to her, she was not influenced by Kathryn Kuhlman's rhetoric.

In Africa in 1954, Usha had fallen from a tree. The accident crushed the joint of her right leg where it meets the hip socket. Surgery, which was performed in London, did not help; she could not lift her leg, and she was able to walk only with a severe limp. A second surgery, in India, also failed to correct the condition. Kathryn Kuhlman's healing message was unintelligible to Usha, but just before Kuhlman began announcing that healings were occurring, Usha felt something in her hip and down her leg that caused her to respond with surprise.

Guided to the stage with her sister-in-law to act as interpreter, Usha Tripathi ran, leaped, and pirouetted before a delighted Kathryn Kuhlman, who stressed to the crowd that "God doesn't care if you're a Catholic, a Jew, or a Hindu." Usha Tripathi could lift her leg for the first time in eighteen years.

Usha returned to her apartment and excitedly woke her husband. He told me what happened:

"She was very excited, and with devils dancing in her eyes she folded her legs and sat Hindu fashion on the floor. It was the first time she could do such a thing since the accident."

Her husband was cautious about accepting the healing as complete, however. He said, "I have asked her not to overdo the running and jumping. I will wait and see; if she can still do these things in six months' time, I will accept that she is healed."

As of this writing, four months after the healing, the effect appears permanent. Usha walks with only a slight limp. Prior to the healing she dragged her leg quite noticeably.

I asked if it was possible that she had had a mental block that prevented her from lifting her leg, but her relatives said that her surgeons cited physical damage as the problem.

I checked two other healing claims, but the doctors I called felt that nothing more than drama was involved. Marion Nelson had surgery on three vertebrae by one of the world's leading specialists. On stage with Kathryn Kuhlman she bent over several times and touched her ankles, exclaiming as she did: "My doctor said I would never be able to do this again."

Her doctor said he did not tell Marion Nelson any such thing; he insisted that the surgery he performed on her back was designed to allow her to bend but that he advised her not to try too soon.

Mildred Moore claimed that she was cured of "incurable" scleroderma. Her doctor has a heavy case load, and he works in more than one clinic. Her records were not examined, but from memory alone the doctor said that he believed Ms. Moore "may have dramatized her ailment."

Whenever faith healing is probed, our national fixation with money gets into the act and clouds the issue. Newspapers cover the healing sessions, and many articles dwell on the large-denomination bills dropped into the circulating baskets. A remark by Angelo Laurie may put the money issue in proper perspective:

"I've paid doctors more in these nine years than Miss Kuhlman raised in both nights put together. And my wife *still* had pain."

Though commercialism in faith healing isn't a scientific issue, it is a philosophical issue. To my knowledge Kathryn Kuhlman has not been accused of profiteering with her healing abilities to the extent that Tony and others have, but some allegations have doubtless been made.

Is there any similarity between the healing ministry of Kathryn Kuhlman and the psychic surgery of the Philippines? Kuhlman would say only that God works through all healers. The talents of Agpaoa and Kuhlman are all part of the same process, and their work takes place on the vital body under the direction of a decarnate human intelligence, which understands the mechanics of both the physical and etheric levels of existence. However, any hint that spiritual entities are involved or that she may be connected with mediumship will bring an emphatic denial from Kathryn Kuhlman and her followers.

One particular aspect of Kathryn Kuhlman's ministry has a direct counterpart among Filipino ritual, the phenomenon I call the "spiritual zap" sessions. Filipino healers enjoy needling their followers with the invisible but painful shots in the arm. They call it "spiritual injection." Kuhlman delivers a spiritual zap equally as mystifying and slightly more impressive when she merely touches another person, without any apparent physical force, and sends him sprawling.

I have not experienced this spiritual knockout touch, but I watched as Kathryn Kuhlman literally floored hundreds of people simply by placing her fingers on their necks near the jawline. During her spring session she seemed to really enjoy rapidly moving from person to person knocking them down in rapid succession. Her attendants are alert, and whenever she puts her hands on someone, one of them rushes behind the recipient in order to catch the falling body and guide it gently to the floor. The unusual zap does not affect everyone in the same way. In the August performance one woman who was felled in this manner did not recover for several minutes.

Skeptics claim that she simply touches pressure points, in

much the same way a karate expert accomplishes this phenomenon. Such claims are absurd: in the first place, she works much too fast to study each patient; and second, pressuring would not propel the person backward as if he had been shoved violently.

Dr. Motoyama described the mysterious Filipino injections as coming from "etheric needles" formed on the ends of the healers' fingertips. Though he makes no overt claims that he is a "clairvoyant," Dr. Motoyama evidently has the ability to perceive other levels of existence. This skill probably stems from his training and function as a Shinto priest. From all the information so far available it can be inferred that Kathryn Kuhlman's spiritual zap is literally a vital body knockdown, accomplished by a spirit entity.

Some researchers have visited Kuhlman's sessions in the company of clairvoyants, who claim to have observed a "number of spirit entities" working in the audience.

It is apparent from testimony and available evidence that the healings commence prior to Kuhlman's startling announcements. Therefore, it is inferred that she receives the information from her source when healing effects have already taken place. Based upon what we know of telepathy, it is possible that her mind receives the information from the minds of those being healed. But what intelligence accounts for the healing itself?

Kathryn Kuhlman emphatically denies any connection to mediumship, and Tony Agpaoa refuses to divulge the identity of his "protector-comforter" on the grounds that it is not yet time to do so. This statement leads many to believe that he will announce someday that he works directly under the influence of some saint. However, Dr. Motoyama has, he says, "observed" Tony's guiding entity. He stated that the guide usually works from a distance, but when he and Tony meditated together in a shrine, the clairvoyant perceived an entity over the healer's shoulder. "It was a male entity, perhaps a primitive Filipino figure," he reported.

Some people have placed Tony on a demigod's pedestal. Rosita told me that he has a half million followers, and the church continues to grow. On his letterhead Tony refers to himself as the "pontifex maximus."

Psychic surgery is a direct by-product of the major phenomenon of mediumship. Mediumship has various tones of meaning to different people, so for the purposes of explaining this hypothesis we will use this definition: a medium is an incarnate person used by a decarnate being.

There are all kinds of mediums and forms of mediumship, ranging from Ouija board communication to trance conversationalists. Every form, however, is basically a one-way communication and function in which the decarnate entity has control.

This thesis does not discount the obvious omnipresent power of God; nor does it discount the abilities of some rare individuals to function on more than one plane of existence with conscious control. But such individuals are not mediums.

Edgar Cayce, the renowned American trance medium, is a perfect example of the mechanics of this phenomenon. While in a deep state of trance, identical to somnambulism in hypnosis, Cayce made fantastic statements regarding healing and geological prophecy. As the incarnate Ego known as Edgar Cayce he was exceptionally spiritual and displayed some psychic abilities, but it was as the medium for decarnate entities that he became famous.

At no time did Cayce exhibit control over the entity using him. Gladys Davis Turner, Cayce's secretary for many years, recalled a number of occasions in which she was concerned that Cayce might not "come out of the trance."

Tony Agpaoa and the other Filipino healers are mediums. Tony does not go into a deep state of trance, however. His control is manifested through his hands and arms, much like a person working the Ouija board. With the guidance of spirit entities he is able to perform phenomenal psychic surgery. When his spirits are not willing, he cannot operate. If Agpaoa were in conscious control of his own "overself" (Mind from the fourth plane of existence) as his followers claim for him, he would not require the aid of decarnate entities to operate on the vital bodies of individuals, and there would be fewer inconsistencies in his abilities.

Rosita and the official church statements of Tony's organization reject the idea of mediumship, claiming that Tony has the power to tap consciously into a level of intelligence, which they call the "Holy Spirit." Many people accept this claim because Tony appears to be fully conscious when he works. However, he admits that he has no control over his hands. Except for the obvious inconsistency in the man and the way he performs, his claim could hardly be refuted on an objective basis.

I have deliberately used the plural when writing of Tony's spirit guides. He claims to have one "protector-comforter" and to work only under this guidance. Many mediums have had one "guide" but were used by several decarnate entities. It is apparent from the varied styles of operating exhibited by Tony over the past several years that he has different controlling intelligences. In Harold Sherman's movies of Tony, taken in 1966, the healer's working style is totally different from his present modus operandi. When I pointed this out to Tony, he did not answer. Rosita replied for him: "There are many ways to heal, and we can use them all. Tony has learned more since then."

His present style is not as spectacular as was his former style, and since Tony is such a showman, it is unreasonable that he would voluntarily choose a less impressive approach. Were he in control, he would surely opt for more flamboyant methods.

Though this principle is manifested in a different way, it is essentially the same with Kathryn Kuhlman. If something as powerful as the Western concept of God or the Holy Spirit were working with her, surely more people would be cured. At the Aire Crown Theater I looked at row upon row of pitiful faces in the wheel-chair area. Many invalids, as believing and faithful as any other, were not touched by the healing spirit.

The Judeo-Christian God is *consistent*. If there's a reason for everything in His creation, there's a reason for man to use his mind, not to accept something on blind faith. Humans have

the qualities of mind that set them apart from the rest of creation. It is said by some that it is in the inherent qualities of mind
that man is created in the image of his creator. Man is endowed
with the same mental qualities as his creator; the gift of mind
was received in a totally undeveloped state, and it's up to the
individual to use the gift in order to develop it.

Spirit entities and physical entities are much the same insofar
as developed mind is concerned. Some dispute this fact and
believe that when we die, we become all-knowing souls. However, there is no evidential basis for this belief. On the other
hand, there is an abundance of evidence for survival of the
entity after death. Why would we be any smarter simply by
leaving our physical shell?

Psychic surgeons and other healers are mediums because they
exhibit human inconsistency rather than God-like perfection.

Those who know—or pretend to know—the secrets of psychic
surgeons whisper that Tony Agpaoa, who was once among
the greatest of healers, is now losing his touch. "He can no
longer do all the things he did," they say.

"Tony's Angel has fallen. It won't be long before he will lose
everything," commented Robert Stent, the Australian healer of
Baguio.

"I worked with Tony; he's losing it," was the unequivocal
statement by Jim Voeks, a twenty-five-year-old resident of San
Francisco who finished his training as a healer under David
Oligani while we were there.

Morris Dreyfus, who greatly admires Tony and credits him
with remarkable healing powers, admitted: "When we were at
Mercado's and Tony was operating on a native girl, he had his
hands inside, but he didn't bring them out. He yelled something
to Mercado in their native language, and the other healer came
running over to take Tony's place. Tony was unable to close,
and it was obvious the experience shook him."

Part of the legend that has built up around Tony claims that
he knows when a patient is going to die and is forewarned
not to operate. It is claimed that his hand changes color as a
warning signal. The change is imperceptible to others, but Tony

sees it clearly. His warning system is apparently slipping; a number of his 1972 patients died after he informed them they were cured.

The following is taken from a letter written by Tony to Laurette Dempsey, whose husband died of cancer of the parotid gland a month after operations performed by Tony in Baguio:

"Concerning your questions in your letter, here are the answers: The doctor's recommendation will help a lot, so go ahead with more cobalt treatment.

"I'm sorry, but there are no more medications that I could send you.

"Yes, there are some more small tumors, and they are subject to cobalt treatment. Yes, you should accept that surgery. That will do good for the tooth. . . .

"Don't you ever worry so much for your dad [husband]. He will be all right in a few more weeks and times. Just continue having faith in Him, and never lose hope. I will continue sending him my absent spiritual healing every 9:00 P.M. of his time. This will help him from his ailment. . . ."

The letter is dated June 13, 1972. Al Dempsey died June 26. Tony is not blamed for the death, but the fact that he didn't know and didn't level with Laurette Dempsey does not strengthen his claims of psychic power.

Other incidents, with an almost comical touch, are reported by two families who visited Tony on separate trips.

The wife of a Chicago restaurant owner was leaving Baguio after successful surgery by Tony when she gashed her foot at the airport. Without hesitating Tony reached down and touched the profusely bleeding cut, and it stopped bleeding instantly. It was a deep laceration, but by the time the plane was in the air, it was healing.

On the other hand, a real estate dealer visited Tony "because I believed in it enough to go but was skeptical enough to want to see proof." Upon arrival at Tony's home, the realtor fell into a construction hole and injured his ankle. He was cut and bruised when he was carried into Tony's home.

"Do you think he put his magic hands on me and fixed me up? Hell no, he used Merthiolate and bandages. Some wonder healer!" the realtor complained.

Such conflicting facts hardly inspire confidence, nor do they testify to a great healing power. Rather the reports point to human inconsistency, which is almost always accentuated whenever the phenomenon of mediumship is involved.

Persons who dabble with mediumship tend to lose the fine edge of their ability to deal with physical reality. Memory lapses are common, and the awareness of future consequences is dulled. One businessman complained:

"Tony is totally irresponsible; he seems to go out of his way to make you disbelieve. I was three days getting an appointment that had been scheduled for eight in the morning of the first day. When I tried to talk to him about it, I might as well have talked to the moon."

This complaint is not uncommon. Many times potential patients would have left in disgust were it not for the great distance they traveled and the expense they incurred. Defenders will say that Tony's forgetting appointments is due to his heavy workload, but busy people are usually efficient people. To attribute his everyday business lapses to the problems of language and custom also falls short—language and custom would create a consistent problem, but Tony is not consistently unreliable. The evidence points clearly to symptoms of mediumship.

Not being a part of the physical plane, the spirit entity evidently tends to overlook some obvious problems for the healer it uses. Why else would an astute man like Tony foster a deliberate hoax when a child could detect it?

When Tony perpetrated the fraud about removing the screws and plate from Mrs. Steinberg's hip, were he in conscious control he certainly would have been aware that she would seek medical verification. There was no pressure applied to get Tony to operate on the hip, so why did he do something so damaging to himself?

Henry Belk made this observation about spirit entities: "They don't eat, they don't pay taxes, and they supply the labor."

What Henry didn't say was that they aren't available when the flak for their mistakes lands on the shoulders of the healer.

While Tony's behavior does not determine definitely that he is a medium, there is no doubt about the late José Arigo, Brazil's famed psychic surgeon. Arigo's facial characteristics changed when he became entranced, and though consciously he knew only his native Portuguese, he spoke in fluent German. His spirit guide, or control, was readily identified as Dr. Fritz, who performed thousands of fantastic healings through the chunky Brazilian medium.

Arigo gets the credit for being a wonder healer, but the effort, the knowledge, and the ability belonged to an intelligence other than his. When performing their operations, the healers are virtually robots.

Arigo is credited with treating more than two million people between 1954 and 1967. As his fame began to spread, he was killed in an auto accident. He often said that he was merely an instrument. "The source of the healing power is Christ and his forces in the spirit world," he said. Arigo learned of his power from Dr. Fritz, who "introduced him to his mission and is always present when Arigo works."

In the December, 1967, issue of *Fate* a headline over the article about Arigo authored by Gene Klinger reads: "Among the myriad mysteries of the Brazilian healings not the least are his personality, language, and appearance changes."

The mediumship was fostered, as it is with many healers, when Arigo was a child. Unlike many mediums, Arigo showed few controversy-provoking inconsistencies. Dr. Fritz evidently took better care of his medium than Tony's entities have for him.

According to the same philosophy that describes the vital body, there are "social" strata on the astral level, in which spirit entities reside. To establish a rapport for mediumship an entity must interlock the spirit and physical planes. It is said this rapport is most readily established between the "lower" astral and the physical. It is also said that the lower astral is the dwelling place for undesirable individuals. A hateful, fearful, mean,

P

negative individual who dies gravitates to the lower astral just as naturally as a positive, cheerful, virtuous individual gravitates to the "lighter" level.

A spirit entity has the same free will possessed by an incarnate entity. Therefore, a gifted physician, if he so chooses, may gravitate from the more distant levels and seek a medium in order to carry out his benevolent services, as in the case of Dr. Fritz and Arigo.

There are numerous examples of considerate, benevolent entities affiliating with mediums, and these are the rare mediums who gain fame. For every famous medium, however, there are ten thousand hapless individuals residing in asylums tagged with the label "hopelessly insane." Those on the physical level are at the distinct disadvantage of not being able to size up the entities who seek to use them as mediums. A Hell's Angel could establish a rapport and tell you that he's St. Michael; if he's clever, you would not know the difference—until inconsistency appeared to make it clear. It is said that if you're standing alone on a mountaintop and you hear a voice, you will listen.

When I asked Dr. Motoyama what he believed the level of the entities operating the healers to be, he replied: "Witch level." This is his term for the level of intellect that desires control over others and seeks physical plane attention despite abiding on a different plane of existence.

Anyone observing Tony's flare for showmanship when the hands over which he has no control are busy operating can readily see that the entity enjoys the astonishment registered by the onlookers.

The entities involved in psychic surgery are not necessarily evil, at least not in the sense that they are out to harm someone. Truly evil entities possess and occupy the asylums.

According to one philosophy, spirit guides are still somewhat on a physical plane ego trip, much as a spirit that haunts and becomes a ghost is traumatically attached to the physical level. Were a spirit guide to do something evil, such as kill a patient, the guide would defeat its purpose because the medium would no longer draw adoring crowds.

It is quite possible that Tony once associated with a benevolent entity who consistently performed unquestionable psychic surgery and protected his medium by warning against interference with karma or imminent death of the patient, but when Tony commercialized the healings, this entity abandoned him to others less meticulous about caring for the problems of the medium. "His Angel has fallen," the people said.

This passing around of the controls is easily verifiable. A hypnotist, who has the same control over his subject as an entity has over his medium, can pass the control around from one person to another while the subject is in trance, and the subject has no authority in the transaction.

In the case of psychic surgery it would be insanity for an unskilled illiterate to play doctor. He'd kill patients through his medium; indeed, this happened to one Filipino healer, who was charged with bleeding a patient to death with over four hundred nail punctures. A spirit trained in medicine while incarnate and able to perceive the vital body function as a decarnate can perform successful psychic surgery.

In order to establish the mediumistic rapport the entity needs a willing subject. Most people have an intuitive feeling that warns them away from giving up conscious control of themselves, but there are evidently a number of channels that can break down these natural defenses. In the instances of Tony and Arigo, the mediumship was established when they were quite young. Apparently asceticism is a sure way to open channels; passivity is another. As youths both Agpaoa and Mercado visited a "sacred" mountain and fasted to "accept the power." Dr. Motoyama pointed out that the Filipinos consider two mountains to be sacred. Apparently a number of entities choose to wait there for potential mediums. One of the mountains is Mt. Arayot, in Huk country.

It is claimed that psychic surgery can be taught. Tony claims to have taught Marcello; Mercado claims to have taught Tony; Simbel claims to have taught Stent, and so on. Many Americans, such as Rosita Rodriguez and Jim Voeks, have studied under a healer. But if a healer has no control, what and how can he teach? Teaching this phenomenon means helping another open channels for mediumship.

Finally, one must consider the loss of energy symptoms exhibited by all mediums. Evidently to make the phenomenon work, the vital forces from an incarnate person—or a number of incarnate persons—are required. The Kirlian photographs from UCLA clearly show the loss of this energy by the healer. Every medium becomes physically exhausted after being used.

These mechanics of mediumship have been presented in an oversimplified form, but essentially this is how psychic surgery works.

I am often asked: "Would you go to one of the healers if you needed surgery?"

Were I in need of healing or surgery, I wouldn't hesitate to travel to the Philippines, but because of the inconsistency, I cannot recommend the healers to others. Each of us has free will and the ability to reason. We must make our own decisions on the basis of available information. In this book I have presented factual information. If you need medical help, the choice between psychic surgery in the Philippines and orthodox medicine at home is yours alone. Neither faith healing, psychic surgery, nor modern medicine is 100 percent certain in every case. It seems only logical that as a last resort, after physicians have declared a patient incurable in their opinions, one has nothing to lose by visiting a faith healer or taking an extended vacation to the Philippines.

The most important lesson I learned from researching psychic surgery is that it is essential to practice the virtue of discrimination. We must all be discerning in our daily lives. That which is *believed* isn't necessarily true. That which is *apparent* isn't necessarily true. Whatever is true, however, withstands every assault of "rationality."

The phenomenon called psychic surgery is genuine. It is accomplished because human beings have an utterly fantastic resource called Mind. The powers and abilities of Mind are only partially known, even by many metaphysicians. When Tony

Agpaoa told us: "I merely plant the seed with my surgery. The patient's mind does the rest," he was telling the truth. If a surgery is faked by the healer or the decarnate entity manipulating the healer and the patient's ultraconsciousness accepted it, the patient's mind would heal the patient's body. Decarnate entities working with the healers understand this fact, and they understand the mechanics for getting the patient's mind to work on the vital body and complete the physical healing. It is an obviously complicated and multifaceted process, which we can all come to understand if we maintain a scientific openmindedness.

Incarnate or decarnate, our minds make us what we are. While incarnate our sickness or health can be influenced by our thoughts. Every individual has been equally "gifted" by God—with the gift of mind. The same mental qualities are available to every human being; in this way we are created equal, in the image of our creator. We differ in the application of these qualities.

When coping with the many mysteries of the universe, we may *choose* to use our minds in order to "distinguish the excellent and the appropriate; to judge between what is good and what is better." Neither blind faith nor the foolish belief in phenomena will unravel universal truths. We gain knowledge and wisdom, and thus spiritual growth, through exercising our own inherent qualities of mind. Learning this lesson is the real value of exploring "unexplained" phenomena such as psychic surgery.

We can contemplate our greatest natural resource—our minds—and apply a great aphorism to our daily lives and to our troubled world:

"Physician, heal thyself."